CW00631571

Translation-mediated Communication in a Digital World

TOPICS IN TRANSLATION
Series Editors: Susan Bassnett, *University of Warwick, UK* and Edwin Gentzler, *University of Massachusetts, Amherst, USA*
Editor for Translation in the Commercial Environment: Geoffrey Samuelsson-Brown, *University of Surrey, UK*

Please contact us for the latest book information:
Multilingual Matters, Frankfurt Lodge, Clevedon Hall,
Victoria Road, Clevedon, BS21 7HH, England
http://www.multilingual-matters.com

TOPICS IN TRANSLATION 23
Editor for Translation in the Commercial Environment:
Geoffrey Samuelsson-Brown, *University of Surrey*

Translation-mediated Communication in a Digital World

Facing the Challenges of Globalization and Localization

Minako O'Hagan and David Ashworth

MULTILINGUAL MATTERS LTD
Clevedon • Buffalo • Toronto • Sydney

Library of Congress Cataloging in Publication Data
O'Hagan, Minako
Translation-mediated Communication in a Digital World: Facing the Challenges of
Globalization and Localization/Minako O'Hagan and David Ashworth
Topics in Translation: 23
Includes bibliographical references and index
1. Translating and interpreting–Data processing. 2. Translating and interpreting–
Technological innovations. 3. Internet. I. Ashworth, David. II. Title. III. Series
P308.O37 2002
418'.02'0285–dc21   2001055823

British Library Cataloguing in Publication Data
A catalogue entry for this book is available from the British Library.

ISBN 1-85359-581-0 (hbk)
ISBN 1-85359-580-2 (pbk)

Multilingual Matters Ltd
UK: Frankfurt Lodge, Clevedon Hall, Victoria Road, Clevedon BS21 7HH.
USA: UTP, 2250 Military Road, Tonawanda, NY 14150, USA.
Canada: UTP, 5201 Dufferin Street, North York, Ontario M3H 5T8, Canada.
Australia: Footprint Books, PO Box 418, Church Point, NSW 2103, Australia.

Copyright © 2002 Minako O'Hagan and David Ashworth.

All rights reserved. No part of this work may be reproduced in any form or by any
means without permission in writing from the publisher.

Typeset by Wordworks Ltd.
Printed and bound in Great Britain by the Cromwell Press Ltd.

Contents

Introduction

What This Book is About

The continually evolving network of computers and telecommunications devices, called the Internet, now provides the context for communication across borders and across cultures. Organizations are using the Internet as a platform for global electronic commerce (e-commerce). Individuals can join forum groups, bulletin boards and chats on topics of interest, and thus communicate with people around the world. By participating in these interactions and creating a Web site or Web page, an individual or institution automatically establishes a visibility to an international public – an opportunity to reach anyone with access to the Internet from anywhere. In this way, the Internet is accelerating the process of globalization. Despite such visibility, however, language continues to be a principal obstacle to full globalization: if an individual or institution wishes to reach speakers of other languages, its contents must be translated or, in the case of voice communication, interpreted.

The process of recreating Web sites in specified language versions is known as Web localization, and it is the fastest-growing area in the translation sector today. The term 'localization' was originally applied to creating regional versions of computer software. The software localizer works directly with the computer language or code in which the software is written, and therefore must have sufficient knowledge to be able to communicate effectively with the client engineers, and to be involved in testing of the localized products. Similarly, with Web site localization, it is necessary to be able to work with HTML, XML and other kinds of formatting tags, including multimedia components such as JPEG images and RealAudio files.

The traditional forms of language support we have known as translation and interpretation are faced with new challenges that come from the new contexts for human communication and interactions afforded by technology.[1] Furthermore, new modes of communication over the Internet are continuing to develop: from static text on computer screens, to short messages on cell phone displays and personal digital assistants, from e-mail to synchronous chat in text or voice. Some of these forms of communication resemble those of the age of the typewriter and the fax machine, but many also incorporate animation, video and other forms of multimedia. The core difference lies in the shift to the digital world which affords all kinds of flexibility in electronic processing.

This multiplicity of types of electronic documents defines a new kind of literacy, variously called electronic or digital literacy. Electronic documents follow a digital life cycle, which is different from the process involved in paper-based contents. Certain contents such as multimedia or voice mail are created electronically from beginning to end, often in forms that would not be possible otherwise. Very large manuals for the operation of equipment such as aircraft, tractors and other heavy equipment, most of which are subject to regular updating, are now published in digital format, be it CD-ROM or online distribution. This in turn allows the use of computer-based translation tools such as translation memory (TM), which compares a new source text against its previous version and allows recycling of previous translations for the applicable portion. In this way, electronic documents have a great compatibility with language engineering.

At present, e-commerce companies express an urgent demand for accurate, appropriate, timely, high-volume translation to localize their Web sites in multiple languages. Similarly, people who use Web sites stumble into language barriers and seek language assistance, since not all Web pages are available in their language. In order to meet such demands, some have turned to engineering solutions: new applications have been developed to allow real-time browsing of Web pages with automatic translation of Web sites, e-mail messages or search engine results. However, many users have learned that machine translation (MT) will rarely satisfy all of their varying communication needs. Those who are heavily involved in MT development and utilization admit the necessity of preparing documents before they are translated (pre-editing) in order to guarantee reasonable results. In the same way, people who use these new modes of communication over the Internet are beginning to realize that they must control the kind of language that they use when they intend to communicate across languages. This is part of the internationalization process that facilitates the ensuing localization/translation process by eliminating, right at the start of the product development cycle, any factors that are likely to hinder globalization. Content management thus becomes a crucial issue in the preparation of documents that will have international visibility. This process may sometimes involve extensive culturalization of contents, including certain non-verbal elements such as icons and layouts, to make the presentation more suitable for the target culture. As a result, new businesses/consultancies are emerging to provide information on cultural differences that can be used in preparing such communications. All of this implies that translators need to acquire a new set of skills and new knowledge. The so-far text-centric Internet has not affected interpreters' working mode in any significant manner. However, the development of voice-communication over the Internet with technologies such as VOIP (Voice Over Internet Protocol) as well as the convergence of mobile phones and the Internet suggest the need to prepare for remote interpreting where all communicating parties are geographically distributed. These emerging technologies, and the need for multilingual support for both text and voice to reach audiences beyond one's own language and cultural boundaries, all work to redefine the translator and interpreter, both in terms of their roles in providing language support, and in the kinds of knowledge and skills that digital literacy requires.

We refer to this emerging field of multilingual support in digital environments as teletranslation and teleinterpretation. In this book we examine the new contexts of communicating, the new literacy, the new requirements for the teletranslator and teleinterpreter and the kinds of tools and training that can facilitate their work.

Origins of the Book and Authors' Perspective

This book is a culmination of our joint thinking over the last few years. The first point of contact the two authors made was through a publication by O'Hagan in 1996 (*The Coming Industry of Teletranslation*). Since then we have collaborated in exchanging ideas and conducting experiments using a variety of new communication modes on the Internet. We are both fascinated by the impact of the new communications media on translation and interpretation. In addition to the extensive teaching experience on translation and language of David Ashworth, and the communication-research involvements with high-tech environments of Minako O'Hagan, who has a translator background, each author has been exposed to the forefront of language industry developments. David has been consulting for a budding Web localization company operating on the Internet, while Minako has close links with the Localization Industry Standards Association (LISA). In 1999 David developed and offered a Web-based online course for Japanese and Chinese translation and Minako attended the course as a student. David continues to give such courses from Hawaii.

Our most recent joint project was a pilot course on teletranslation and teleinterpretation run by courtesy of the Global Virtual University (GVU). The GVU, developed by Professor Emeritus Tiffin of Victoria University of

Wellington, New Zealand, hosted our ten-week course between September and November 2000 with a weekly live voice session based on a VOIP platform. This allowed us to explore our ideas relating to teletranslation and teleinterpretation with an international group of students and in an emerging technological environment for pedagogical purposes. The pilot course pointed us to the areas of our own weaknesses and also those of the technology. For example, at the time of writing, VOIP platforms are not sufficiently reliable for conducting classes that depend solely on the voice channel. For the same reason, simultaneous teleinterpretation in this environment is not yet feasible. However, the course also helped us to crystallize a number of concepts that we consider are significant for translators and interpreters to survive and thrive in the Internet era. For example, while teletranslation is already in operation, with translators receiving and delivering work on the Net, the full implications of digital communication are not well understood. As for teleinterpretation over the Internet, it is yet to develop into a commercial service owing to the unstable technology. And yet, after conducting classes using a VOIP application, we could clearly see its potential. With the convergence of voice and Web progressing with the third generation (3G) mobile technology, we believe that remote interpreting in one form or another will become a necessity in the near future. Our conviction is that both translators and interpreters who are trained in and accustomed to the analog/atomic environment need to raise awareness for the emerging digital/virtual environment, which changes a number of basic assumptions for their work.

Several textbooks and references, plus numerous Internet documents, have appeared on the areas of localization and language engineering. In particular, they cover issues in software localization with some addressing Web localization (see, for example http://www.multilingualwebmaster. com). The press and online literature on MT is abundant, and goes back almost fifty years. In this book, we wish to stay close to the present and emerging developments in electronic communication across languages, but avoid covering the same ground as others. We expect to provide a fresh perspective on the future of translation and interpretation in light of the new context in which these professions need to operate. We also note a certain lack of Asian perspective in the area of writing on recent developments in translation and interpretation. For example, publications on localization seem to be dominated by Western perspectives (although they may discuss the processes involved in localizing into Asian languages). Both of us being Japanese speakers and thoroughly familiar with the cultural aspects, we hope to add an Eastern perspective to the treatment of the topic, which may be useful in maintaining the balance of the globalization equation seen from 'the other' side.

As we write, technologies are constantly changing. This is the unfortunate mismatch between the static print media we employ and the dynamic technology that this book talks about. This dilemma has been expressed by Negroponte (1995) who published *Being Digital* on paper. To deal with this conflict, our approach is to indicate the areas of ignorance and offer our suggestions for filling in the gap rather than to provide fast and set knowledge to well-defined problems. In doing so, we hope that readers are able to retain awareness of their ignorance as new developments take place and will formulate their own strategies to cope with them. In today's technological environment, we have to be prepared to accept that we are aiming at moving targets. If this book can provide a framework to effectively deal with future challenges for the parties who are involved in the field of language support, we have succeeded in conveying our message.

Our Approach and the Scope of the Book

Our main hypothesis is that technological changes affecting communication modes are going to profoundly impact on the professions of translators and interpreters to such an extent that new professions will result. Our assumption is that new modes of communication employed across languages will both drive and enable new types of language support. But this book is not about technological predictions. Particularly under the current pace of technological innovations, it is almost impossible to predict precisely into what form today's Web will develop in five years' time, or to know the exact shape into which mobile communication technology will advance in interaction with the Internet. In full recognition of such unpredictability, we will take the approach of futures research, which accepts uncertainties but facilitates cognisance of factors relevant to future developments of the subject under study. In our case, the relevant factors are the newly-emerging communications contexts in which translation and interpretation need to function.

New domains such as localization are only just beginning to be included in translation programmes by educational institutions despite the fact that localization is becoming an indispensable language support function. In our attempt to explore the nature of the change taking place in translation and interpretation, we have found that localization provides an excellent case for theorizing the emerging paradigm. Localization, particularly in the light of globalization, encompasses a wider range of aspects than merely the message itself, which is subject to language support. Instead of focusing on the translating and interpreting process in isolation, we have therefore endeavoured to examine the entire context of communication involved in the transaction of translation and interpretation. To allow this perspective, we have taken communicative approaches by applying communication models of translation such as those developed by Nida and Taber (1969) and Gile (1995). Communication models have enabled us to take into account the sender and the receiver of the message subject to translation or interpretation. Further, we have introduced a framework which we call 'Translation-mediated Communication' (TMC) in association with CMC (Computer-mediated Communication). This approach seems to us to be particularly suitable for our treatment of translation and interpretation that are involved in multilingual CMC over the Internet.

Another important path that we follow in this book is an ignorance-based and learner-oriented approach whereby awareness of the problem is raised and each learner is able eventually to arrive at a solution on his or her own accord, depending on the context in which problems need to be dealt with. Instructors using this book as a text book may find that this approach drives an instructional methodology that is exploratory and collaborative rather than pre-determined and teacher-dependent. Such characteristics seem to fit in with positive dimensions that virtual learning environments are embracing, as identified by a number of experts (e.g. Kiraly, 2000b; Warschauer, 1999).

To the extent that we deal with emerging technological environments, we accept that the scope of this book is limited. Many of the observations we make may be considered intuitive and subjective. Nevertheless, we hope they may illuminate the nature of changes taking place in the field of translation and interpretation, and allow readers to draw their own conclusions in their search for new paradigms of translation and interpretation. In the spirit of coming to grips with an emerging and constantly evolving field, we append questions and research ideas at the end of each chapter.

Readership of the Book

This book is written with three main groups of readers in mind. The first group are practising translators who are increasingly concerned with the rapidly developing communications media and their implications for their work, and who want to take advantage of the global marketplace opening up on the Internet. The book will address such concerns by focusing on key questions to lead readers into the paradigm of teletranslation. Similarly, the book is intended for practising interpreters who may be conversant in using the Internet to do background research for their assignments but have not experienced remote interpretation, particularly on the Internet with its increasing number of voice platforms.

The second group includes entrepreneurs who wish to provide a language service on the Internet, but are not entirely familiar with the language business, as well as translation managers who are employed from outside the translation sector per se but are nevertheless engaged in multi-faceted language solutions in the global communication environment.

Educators comprise the third category of readership. Teachers of translation and interpretation who wish to address emerging issues concerning the immediate and longer-term future direction of the professions may be alerted to key issues. Given recent attempts to narrow the gap between theory and practice in the training of translators and interpreters, it seems appropriate to face up to the changes taking place and to bring these traditional and well-established professional domains into the future.

Organization of Contents

Given that this book is intended for a mixed audience, we offer here brief guidance on the relevance of chapters to different groups of readers. The book is divided into four main parts under which the emerging context for teletranslation and teleinterpretation is explored.

Part One provides the big picture, highlighting the major changes taking place in translation and interpretation (which we refer to as Translation to include both) with the advent of the Internet. We introduce a new framework Translation-mediated Communication (TMC). Chapter 1 describes the traditional function of Translation on the basis of TMC, and highlights issues arising from a newly emerging context in which Translation has to function. Chapter 2 concentrates on a number of specific attributes of the emerging context in the shift to teletranslation and teleinterpretation. The new context includes key concepts such as digital literacy, particularly in light of translation and translator competence. Changes are also considered by describing Translation as a communication system.

Part Two concentrates on technologies, which are both driving and enabling new forms of Translation, together with wider implications of globalization and localization. Chapter 3 looks into natural language processing technologies that have become particularly relevant to the digital communications environment on the Internet. It discusses the developments of language support automation, and tools for translators and interpreters. Chapter 4 turns to technological developments that are driving an underlying change in communications modes, notably Computer-mediated Communication (CMC) modes. On the basis of specific characteristics of the CMC mode, we introduce a potential hybrid language support called transterpreting. Chapter 5 examines how the globalization process is fundamentally affecting Translation, in particular with the need for localization. Building on Gile's (1995) concept of the message consisting of 'Content' and 'Package,' we highlight a new dimension of Translation: culturalization of the message. The chapter discusses the importance of language management in globalization.

Part Three moves to the coalface of Translation practice by focusing particularly on teletranslation and teleinterpretation. Chapter 6 observes how teletranslation is operating and advancing. It highlights key emerging trends towards mature teletranslation. Chapter 7 turns to remote modes of interpretation such as telephone interpreting in relation to the future development of teleinterpretation. A number of critical issues are discussed in the path towards teleinterpretation. Chapter 8 is an examination of the Internet as a platform for professional developments for translators and interpreters in response to new skill and knowledge requirements. It discusses Web-based courses for translators with reference to case studies, and touches on future prospects for such courses for interpreters.

Part Four changes from the present into the future tense. Chapter 9 envisages the role Translation may play in the future information society based on extensive digital communications networks. It examines the emergence of a new paradigm of language support, and provides a number of future scenarios. Chapter 10, the concluding chapter, draws our argument into a vision of teletranslation and teleinterpretation as the future of translation and interpretation and highlights key issues for Translation-mediated Communication.

Notes

1. The traditional forms of translation and interpretation are aptly symbolized by the name of a publisher established more than two decades ago called Pen and Booth, which published books on translation and interpretation, especially education in this field. Perhaps now it would be 'Word Processor and Computer.'

Glossary

An explanation of some of the technical terms in the sense used in this book.

3G (third generation): a new generation of mobile network technology with broadband transmission capabilities.

AIIC (International Association of Conference Interpreters): the international professional association that represents conference interpreters and sets standards for the practice of the profession.

ALPAC (Automatic Language Processing Advisory Committee): the ALPAC report presented to the US Academy of Science in 1965 concluded that machine translation research is futile, virtually bringing MT research to an end particularly in the USA.

ASP (application service provider): any third-party entity that manages and distributes software-based services and solutions to customers remotely via the Internet or a private network.

Asynchronous communication: one-way communication that takes place at a given time.

Avatar: a computer-generated graphical figure typically representing a person in cyberspace with varying degrees of interactivity.

BBS (bulletin board system): a system whereby subscribers can electronically post a message, which in turn can be viewed by the other subscribers.

Browser: a software program that enables one to view Web documents.

Bricks and mortar: a term used to describe the traditional, non Internet-based, business mode that relies on a physical building and transportation.

Chat: an interactive communication mode between two or more people who can enter text by typing on the keyboard, and the entered text appears on the other user's monitor. Today many chat sites also allow voice-based interactions (also see IRC).

Clicks and mortar: a term used to describe a hybrid business mode where both traditional mode and Internet-based mode are used.

CMC (Computer-mediated Communication): communication modes facilitated by computer.

Computer (software) agents/intelligent agent: software program designed to perform user-specified tasks, typically communicating via a message-passing paradigm.

DTP (desktop publishing): a computer application to streamline the documentation process via a desktop computer.

Distributed virtual reality: virtual reality environments that can be shared by multiple parties from different locations.

EBMT (example-based machine translation): a machine translation system that is based on a bilingual database of example phrases derived from a large corpus of texts and their translations.

Emoticon: ASCII symbols used to provide a graphical display of emotions.

Futures research: research that has the primary objective of assisting decision-makers to better understand the potential consequences of present and future decisions by developing images of alternative futures.

Globalization: the process of facilitating localization to allow a product to be used in countries other than the country of its origin.

HTML (hypertext markup language): the text-based language used to construct Web pages.

HTTP (hypertext transfer protocol): a protocol used by computers on the Internet to communicate with each other – specifications used for Web-based interactions to provide a client–server relationship.

Hypertext: text embedding links which in turn can be clicked with a mouse. When the link is clicked, the user is taken to another document or a different section of the current document.

i-mode: NTT DoCoMo's Internet service over mobile phones.

Internationalization: (sometimes shortened to I18N, meaning 'I- eighteen letters-N'): the process of planning and implementing products and services so that they can easily be adapted to specific local languages and cultures, a process called localization.

Internet II: a collaborative effort among a number of universities, US federal R&D agencies, and private sector firms to develop a next-generation Internet for research and education, including enhanced network services as well as multimedia applications.

Intranet: an internal or company-wide Internet network that can be used by anyone who is directly connected to the organization's computer network.

IRC (Internet Relay Chat): a chat system developed by Jarkko Oikarinen in Finland in the late 1980s. To join an IRC discussion, one needs an IRC client and Internet access. The IRC client is a program that runs on the user's computer and sends and receives messages to and from an IRC server.

Java script: a programming language for developing Client Internet applications. The Web browser interprets JavaScript statements embedded in an HTML page.

JPEG: a type of image file used on the Internet. JPEG files are compressed to economize the transmission of normally large files carrying images.

Localization: the process of adapting a product or service to a particular language, culture, and desired local 'look-and-feel.'

Macro, keyboard: instructions to a computer that allocates to one key stroke the automatic typing of repetitive words and phrases.

Media translation and interpreting: translation and interpretation tasks relating to audiovisual media, including subtitling, voice over, narrating or simultaneous interpreting of broadcast contents.

Multiple language vendors (MLV): a localization service provider covering a wide range of languages.

Packet switching: a technique of switching signals whereby the signal stream is broken into packets and reassembled at the destination.

Paradigm shift: Thomas Kuhn used the term to explain scientific revolutions; according to Kuhn a new scientific discovery can be explained only by a new set of assumptions (a new paradigm), therefore causing a paradigm shift.

PDA (personal digital assistant): a handheld device that combines computing, telephone/fax, and networking features.

PDF (portable document format): a universal file format developed by Adobe to allow efficient electronic distribution of documents. PDF files preserve all the fonts, formatting, graphics, and color of any source document, regardless of the application and platform used to create it.

Portal: a Web site that consists of a collection of links to the most popular web services on the Internet.

POTS: traditionally used for 'plain old telephone service' – the basic telephone service. In this book we use the term to mean low value-added **plain old translation service.**

RealAudio: a program that allows sound files to be transmitted from the Internet to the user's PC.

RTF (rich text format): the format developed by Microsoft to enable documents to be transferred between application programs.

Search engine: an information searching system that allows people to search for information on the Internet.

Sight translation: a mode of translation whereby a given text in the source language is read out directly in the target language by the translator or the interpreter.

Simultaneous shipment (simship): a simultaneous release of multiple language versions of a software product.

Single language vendors (SLV): a localization service provider that covers a single or a limited number of languages.

Software publisher: a software house that produces software products.

Synchronous communication: two-way communication that takes place in real-time.

TM (translation memory): a database of previous translations whereby source and target language segments are aligned.

Uni-cast: to transmit information between a single sender and a single receiver over a network, such as when e-mail is sent or a Web browser connects to a home page, thus not economical when sending a high-bandwidth stream such as graphics or video whereas **multi-cast** permits moderately large real-time bandwidths to be efficiently shared by an unconstrained number of hosts.

Unicode: usually used as a generic term referring to a two-byte character-encoding scheme that is designed to accommodate most of the world's languages.

Unification: a system whereby similar characters among Chinese, Japanese and Korean scripts (Han idiographs) are represented by a single character so that the full Han idiographic set fits into the Unicode standard's available code points.

Virtual community: a community created on computer networks which is bound by a common interest in a given topic.

Virtual team: a group of people working from different locations using computer networks.

VOIP (voice over the Internet protocol): specifications that define the transmission of speech over networks using the Internet protocol.

WAP (wireless application protocol): specifications that standardize the way wireless devices can be used for Internet access.

Web phone: mobile phones that can access the Internet.

Whispering mode (interpreting): a mode of interpreting whereby the interpreter whispers interpretation to the given party.

XML (extensible markup language): an enhanced version of HTML.

Chapter 1
Translation and Interpretation in Transition: Serving the Digital World

This chapter establishes the basic function of language facilitation traditionally known as translation and interpretation (*Translation*) and overviews how the Internet is driving the need to communicate globally, in turn making a significant impact on Translation. The Internet is fast becoming a prevalent communications channel across a wide range of economic sectors as well as among individuals. For Internet users, the implication is how to communicate and process information in multilingual and multicultural contexts. For the providers of Translation, the new communications environments are creating a new demand while also enabling new ways of meeting that demand. This chapter introduces the approach based on *Translation-mediated Communication (TMC)* and highlights the issues for Translation arising from the shift from primarily print-based and physical transportation-based communications environments to the digital world.

Translation-mediated Communication (TMC)

Globalization has been an ongoing process for some time, blurring the national boundary of each country with the increasing volume of international movements of people and goods via physical transportation or electronic means, and often by both. One implication of globalization has been increased interactions among people who do not understand one another's language. Cross-border business negotiations or the sale of products in overseas markets have so far required professional language assistance for face-to-face meetings or marketing materials in different languages. Translation (with a capital T), which in this book we use to refer to both translation and interpretation, is primarily called for when language becomes a barrier rather than a means to communication. However, globalization driven by the Internet-based infrastructure is now producing a new set of requirements for Translation. This is because the Internet is changing both the nature of communication that becomes subject to Translation, and the mechanism by which the given communication is transmitted, processed and stored.

In particular, a range of new modes of communication called *Computer-mediated Communication (CMC)* is affecting Translation. In CMC, the computer is a mechanism for exchange of messages. The capacity of the computer, the available software and the bandwidth of transmission, all have an influence on exactly how messages will be exchanged. In other words, the computer may serve as a channel for exchanging messages, and will also shape the communications behavior of the people who use it. Now we add to CMC the possibility of providing both synchronous and asynchronous Translation to the exchange of messages via CMC. We consider the World Wide Web (Web) as accommodating various forms of CMC, including the display of conventional text. See, for example, the results of a search on Google. They may include Acrobat™ PDF files, most of which are conventional text plus graphics, but can also accommodate multimedia files. A special interest, however, is a possibility and the need for Translation to handle any kind of digital content, including real-time audio, video, and computer conferencing (i.e. chat), multimedia, and asynchronous e-mail. Providing multilingual support for CMC thus opens a new kind of language support based on a new literacy that involves digital media.

This is the background behind our use of the term 'Translation-mediated Communication' (TMC) in association with CMC. Any communication facilitated by Translation can be called TMC, but our principal interest is to examine the impact of the Internet as it results in new dimensions of language support traditionally based on print media and physical trans-portation. We use TMC as the framework for our exploration and this in turn means that we take the approach of treating Translation as communication. There are a number of scholars who developed translation models based on Shannon's (Shannon & Weaver, 1949) Mathematical Model of Communication, including Nida & Taber (1969), Bell (1991) and Gile (1995). The simplicity of the Shannon model allows us to illustrate the role of Translation as an embedded function between the sender and the receiver with the Translator acting both as the receiver of the message in the source language and the sender of the message in the target language as described by Nida and Taber (Figure 1.1).

This model highlights the purpose of Translation as 'an act of communication which attempts to relay, across cultural and linguistic boundaries, another act of communication...' (Hatim & Mason, 1997:1). Given that Shannon's model was originally intended for synchronous telephone communication, this model is equally applicable to interpretation, in which the sender and the receiver may be engaged in constant turn taking. The main difference in modus operandi between translation and interpretation resides in the fact that interpretation caters to synchronous communication where all communi-

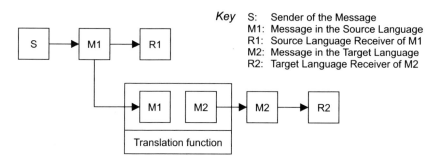

Figure 1.1 Nida and Taber's model (adapted from Nida & Taber, 1969: 23)

cating parties (including the interpreter) are normally present in one physical location and communicate in real-time. By comparison, translation facilitates asynchronous communication via writing with a certain time lag. The translation service therefore tends to be location-independent in relation to the sender and the receiver, whereas interpretation normally requires the interpreter's presence in the given communicative situation. As this model demonstrates, the Translation function is pivotal to the given inter-lingual communication and is inter-dependent on the sender and the receiver as well as the message. However, in reality, the most common notion among Translation clients is that Translation is a stand-alone element that can be added on, and is fundamentally separate from the overall inter-lingual communication process. Given that Shannon's Communication model tends to focus on the transmission function of telecommunications, we will combine our analysis of TMC with Gile (1995), who also uses a communication-based approach but is more focused on the Sender, the Receiver and the Message. Following his convention, we will also capitalize these key terms wherever we are referring specifically to these parties in the context of TMC.

Let us first define our use of terminology. In TMC we define the Sender as the originator of the message (the author of the written message or the speaker of the verbal message in the source language) and the Receiver as the party who receives the message in the target language. In our model, the terms Sender or Receiver do not refer to a translation company or agency who may distribute work to individual translators and interpreters.

The Sender and the Receiver

The Sender initiates a message, which may be in written or spoken form, such as an advertising copy of a product, a latest novel, a film or business negotiation talks. In the context of Translation, the Sender would normally create the Message with the source language Receiver in mind. For example, a novel, technical documentation or product brochure would be written, at least initially, for the source language readers. By comparison, a Sender whose Message requires interpreting would normally assume that at least some Receivers do not share the same language as the Sender. It is most unlikely for TMC with an interpreter to take place without the Sender having foreign language Receivers in mind. The only exceptions are some cases of media interpreting. For example, CNN news, which is produced for an English-speaking audience, may also be transmitted to foreign language Receivers via interpretation (voice over or subtitles). In this case, the Sender of the message is not directly aware of the Receiver in a foreign language.

This also relates to the fact that the most common interpretation modus operandi involves all communicating parties being present at the same physical location so that the Sender naturally knows the presence of the interpreter as well as Receivers who lack source language capability. By comparison, in translation the Sender does not often come face to face with the translator or the Receiver. In fact, some translation problems are caused by the very fact that the Sender of the message does not take the subsequent translation process into consideration. This issue is currently addressed by a process known as internationalization, which takes into account the localization process from the very start of the product development cycle. The next chapter and Chapter 5 deal with this subject in more detail. We hope that the new TMC framework will serve to redefine these terms.

Unlike the Sender, the Receiver in TMC is mostly made aware of the involvement of Translation in the communication process. For example, the audience of a dubbed foreign film knows that the original was in a different language, while readers of foreign novels normally know that they are reading a translated version. Another difference between translation and interpretation lies in the role of the Receiver feedback. While the translator receives no feedback during the translation process, and the subsequent feedback, if any, tends to be delayed, Receiver feedback plays a significant role in interpreting, as it can indicate in real-time how the interpreter's performance is being received. Figure 1.2 shows the interactions among the Sender, the Receiver and the interpreter in a typical small group face-to-face consecutive interpreting situation.

Figure 1.2 illustrates how the Receiver (R2) observes the Message (M1) being delivered by the Sender (S), albeit without understanding the verbal content but taking in some nonverbal communication cues such as facial expressions and body movements (kinesics), although the Receiver (R2) may not 'read' them correctly. This contrasts with the situation for the translator, who normally works in isolation from either the Sender or the Receiver.

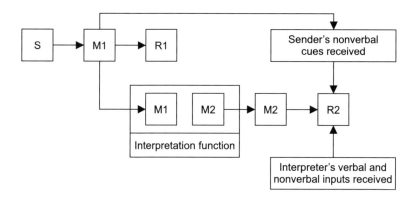

Figure 1.2 TMC for face-to-face interpreting

The Message

The Message is a given communication or information that becomes subject to Translation. In conventional Translation, the Message consists of written texts for translation and speech for interpretation. Gile (1995: 26) sees it consisting of 'content' and 'package'. The term 'package' refers to 'the linguistic and peri-linguistic choices made by the Sender and to the physical medium through which they are instantiated.' According to Gile's definition, in written texts, the package will include words, grammatical structures, fonts, page layout, graphics, etc. For speech, it is made up of the words, grammatical structures, the voice and delivery, as well as nonverbal cues. Content and package interact to affect the message as a whole. As pointed out by Gile, a good content can be weakened by poor style of writing or delivery of speech, and vice versa. In thinking of the change in the nature of the Message with the advent of the Internet, this dual view to analyze the Message becomes relevant to our purposes to highlight the changing nature of the Message.

The Translator

While the Translator is expected to retain the content of the Message intact, in many cases modifications are inevitable. Ingenious transformations are made, not only with literary translations, but also with industrial translations of a technical nature. The Translation process also affects the packaging of the Message, since the Translator practically re-sends the Message in the target language. This is why the translator is expected to be able to write like a scientist when translating a scientific document with appropriate use of technical terminology, and the interpreter is expected to be able to speak like a diplomat when interpreting for diplomatic talks.

Another unique aspect involved in TMC is that the very process of Translation sometimes highlights certain aspects of the Message as detrimental to smooth inter-lingual communication, while those same aspects may not deter the source language receiver (R1) in intra-lingual communication. This is because Translation must take the Message from the source language domain to that of the target language. For example, some ambiguity that does not cause a problem in one language may require clarification before it is expressed in another language. In this sense, the Translator as the intermediary receiver of the message in the source language tends to be much more sensitized to those elements of the Message that are not friendly to the target language or target-culture. Similarly, the interpreter will be much more aware of the speech in terms of coherence than the casual home audience may realize. In other words, the Translator re-shapes the content and the package to fit into the target language and cultural context as expected by the Receiver. However, the Translator is normally limited in terms of the degree of modifications that can be made and the choice of physical medium in which the Message is contained – to two-dimensional text for the translator, and to oral speech for the interpreter. Such tasks as subtitling for films impose further restrictions in terms of the number of characters allowed in translation to fit into the specified space. Translation primarily is work conditioned by the content and the package imposed by the Sender.

From the perspective of the Sender or the Receiver of the Message, the Translator's role is expected to be transparent. However, in reality, this rarely is the case. As pointed out by Gile (1995: 32), 'the Translator is instrumental in helping to achieve the Sender's aims, but cannot guarantee their fulfillment.' This may be evident if one considers communication breakdowns that commonly take place between sender and receiver speaking the same language and sharing the same cultural background. In other words, the successful facilitation of inter-lingual communication is not entirely determined by the performance of the Translator alone, but also is affected by the Sender, the Message and the Receiver. The following section compares monolingual and inter-lingual communication in order to further highlight the function of Translation.

Monolingual versus inter-lingual communication as TMC

Monolingual communication

A necessary condition for successful communication is a sharing of the knowledge upon which to build comprehension. The sender makes assumptions about what the receiver can understand, creates messages based on this assumption, and adjusts further messages on the basis of feedback from the receiver. Alternatively, especially when immediate feedback is not feasible (as in the case of a public lecture), the sender tries to anticipate possible gaps in receiver knowledge by including in his message supplementary information.

Communication will break down if the sender makes incorrect assumptions, and does not receive feedback to enable corrections. It may also break down if the necessary conditions of shared knowledge are obtained but either (1) the sender is inarticulate in presenting the message, or (2) the message is inappropriately packaged in terms of choice of style or register, in particular.

Inter-lingual communication as TMC

TMC succeeds when the conditions for successful communication are met and the Translator understands and conveys the Messages. However, in TMC, the Translator is in danger of being blamed for communication failures, as it is easy to 'blame the translator' when, in fact, the above conditions (between monolinguals) are not met. Of course, communication will fail if the Translator does not understand the Sender, uses inappropriate packaging and the like. Sender and Receiver may lack linguistic sophistication, and fall back on 'objectivist' assumptions about language (and knowledge in general). That is, they (clients, Receivers) can attribute breakdown to the translator 'not knowing the right words.'[1] Gile (1995: Chapter 9) points out, interestingly, that if messages on a complex subject are phrased (packaged) in simple language, and background knowledge is not shared, communication breakdown may very well still occur.

One significant source of failure in inter-lingual communication can stem from incorrect assumptions of common beliefs and experience that actually differ according to cultural background, knowledge, preferences and pragmatics (use of language). A US learner of Japanese may interpret a negative question 'Aren't you going to the theater?' as asking for a yes-or-no answer (seeking facts) when it is an invitation (in context). This is a trivial example of a host of possible types of misinterpretations. Attitudes towards the opposite sex, human rights, obligations of a person who suggests having dinner together (in the Philippines, this could very well be an invitation that the inviter intends to treat the invitees), and so on are examples of the many areas in which misunderstandings and misinterpretations can occur. The Sender cannot be expected to know such differences in cultural background and preferences. A competent Translator, who is aware of the differences and has strategies to deal with them, can minimize communication breakdowns by modifying the Message to make it understandable and appropriate. No other person can do this in TMC. This affects fidelity as narrowly defined as, for example, in judicial interpreting, where the interpreter is required to be as literal as possible, regardless of cultural differences between Sender and Receiver).

The client

Translation, as we are discussing it, in this book is a commercial activity and therefore subject to demands made by the client. We define the 'client' as someone who commissions the task of Translation and therefore is the user of a given Translation service. By comparison, for the purpose of this book, an intermediary (such as a translation agency) who may deal directly with the client and distributes the work to a Translator is considered to be the provider of a Translation service. The client typically sets deadlines, negotiates prices and provides specific conditions such as selective translations and simultaneous interpretation.

Translation client

Translation work may be commissioned by (1) the Sender or (2) the Receiver of the Message.

(1) When the Sender of the Message commissions the translation work, the Message reaches the Receiver in his or her language. Localization is a good example of this, as it attempts to adapt the Message to be suitable to the Receiver of the message. Literary translation is another example of Sender-commissioned translation – it enables the Receiver to read literary works in his or her own language. This pattern tends to take place for information dissemination rather than gathering purposes and a high-quality translation is generally required. However, in this case, the Sender of the Message is typically unable to directly assess the quality of the translation, thus the feedback on translation tends to come from the Receiver (end-user) to the translator normally via the Sender.

(2) When the Receiver commissions the work, it is because the message is received in an unfamiliar language. For example, a Japanese scientist who receives the abstract of a technical paper in German may decide to have it translated into Japanese. In this case, the translation exercise normally does not directly affect the Sender of the Message. This pattern

tends to take place for information-gathering purposes, and may not always require a top-quality translation. Recent applications of machine translation (MT) to browse Web pages in real-time are an example of this – the Receiver of the Message needs a translation, and the quality required is often for 'information only' purposes. In this case, the Receiver is able to provide feedback directly to the provider of the service or the translator, as the target language is the Receiver's language.

Interpretation client

Where interpretation is used to facilitate communication, it may be commissioned by one of the parties involved in the given communication. For example, in a business meeting situation, the interpreter may be briefed from the point of view of the commissioner of the assignment and therefore may be well informed of that party's context of communication. In other instances such as conferences and court cases, the organizers of the conference or the court authority may commission the interpreter. With an interpretation service, because all verbal communication needs to go through the interpreter, both the Sender and the Receiver become the end-users of the service who give feedback, overtly or covertly, to the interpreter.

So far we have established how TMC functions and the roles played by key parties involved in TMC in conventional Translation environments. With the advent of the Internet, however, the basis of TMC is beginning to shift to digital-based communication. The Internet already affects most areas of translation, mainly because the Internet has so far been a text-oriented medium while interpretation remained primarily a location-dependent service. In the next section, we look at the impact of the Internet and its potency.

Impact of the Internet on Translation

Conventional translation markets affected by the Internet

Product and service information has been one of the traditional markets for translation and is now being increasingly made available online. In some cases, such information may be available only online since this saves the physical printing and distribution cost of the paper-based documentation. This in turn means that translations of product brochures, manuals or PR literature are now also published in electronic mode. Similarly, some of the world's major daily newspapers and magazines, which are published online, are often made available on the Web in a number of languages. Unlike printed versions, these online editions are subject to regular and frequent updates, which need to be reflected also in the translated versions.

The time available for translation has therefore been shortened in some cases. Also the readers of online versions of publications may read them on screen rather than on paper, at least initially.

International publishing is a major business sector, which has been leveraged by translation. Recent best sellers such as the _Harry Potter_ series are published in translations into major languages. Many literary translators have commented how e-mail has helped them to access the authors (the Sender of the Message) much more readily and directly than it was possible before, allowing them to resolve translation-related questions quickly.

But the Internet is affecting more fundamentally the form of the book itself. Some popular authors such as Stephen King have been experimenting with releasing new novels exclusively on the Internet with an expectation of payment from online readers (Sachs, 2000). This form of publishing has not yet taken off, but if and when it does, this may suggest that the time available for translation may become even less than that allowed for the print media in order to take advantage of the elimination of production time required for print-based publications and physical distribution. This could mean that translation clients will expect the process to be almost synchronous like 'Just in Time Translation' or 'Translation on Demand.' Furthermore, e-books are being published as online books that are to be read exclusively on the computer screen or some kind of IT device.

The majority of authors who were used to writing on paper now use computers and in the future may never see their manuscript on paper, since the readers will also likely read it on screen. The implication of this is that the translator may be expected to do away with the paper-copy stage altogether. Would this affect the translation process? Also, online texts including e-books are likely to make use of the hypertext features, sometimes including multimedia components. Multimedia hyperlinks could mean that the traditionally text-to-text translation would extend into the realm of multimedia translation, involving sound and images. This will make translation work multimodal. Multimedia developments on the Internet, incorporating TV and radio broadcasts as well as Internet films, also suggest that some areas of media translation and interpretation are likely to move into the Internet.

Table 1.1 summarizes follow-on effects from the Internet on conventional translation markets.

New areas of demand created by the Internet

In addition to the traditional areas of translation being affected by the Internet, entirely new types of language support requirements have risen from the Internet.

Table 1.1 Conventional translation market and the impact of the Internet

Translation Market	Description	Implication of Internet
Product documentation	Documentation for export products ranges from PR materials to user manuals which are subject to translation. These are mainly distributed in paper-based media.	Some customer and product documentation is making inroads into Web sites through which the customers are asked to look up relevant information. In this context, translations are seen on screen rather than on paper (although printing the page is possible). The time available for translation may be reduced.
Local editions of major international publications	Some magazines with a worldwide circulation have been published in separate language editions. They are also often adjusted content-wise to local market interest rather than providing a straight translation of the original edition.	Some of such publications, including major daily newspapers have become available online. Online editions are normally shorter than and different from their printed versions and are subject to frequent updates, demanding a shorter timeframe for translation, and with a wider native-speaker audience.
Literary works	Literary works have been translated all over the world for centuries and will continue to be in the future.	The emergence of e-books and of novels published exclusively on the Internet may not only increase the volume of translation work in this area, but is also likely to reduce the time available for the translation process.
Audio-visual subtitles, dubbing, voice-over	Audio-visual programmes broadcast via TV, films, video or CD have employed language support in the form of subtitling, dubbing or voice-over.	With technical platforms such as RealAudio and streaming techniques, the Internet is absorbing broadcasting, including TV, radio and video and films. This may mean that media translators and interpreters work on the Internet.

Web localization

Of particular significance is the Web, based on which electronic commerce (e-commerce) is rapidly growing and expected to generate global sales in excess of US$3 trillion by 2003 (LISA, 2000). However, as the world becomes a single electronic marketplace, language is becoming an obstinate barrier to communication. English is no longer a universally effective medium of communication in the context of Web-based environments. The majority of Web documents are still in English, however, while the size of the Internet population is forecast to rise to 1 billion by 2005 of which Chinese alone will account for about 300 million. Similarly, the number of online users in Europe is forecast to exceed those in the USA in 2003 (LISA, 2000). In order for the business to take advantage of the emerging worldwide marketplace on the Internet, it clearly needs to speak the customer's language and take into account some of the cultural factors relevant to that particular market. This is now gradually being recognized by the businesses that wish to go global, and this means that e-commerce alone will create specific needs for language support that is functional on the Web or any other platforms that may become available in future.

Web localization is probably the most direct and prominent impact of the Internet so far on translation demand, and is currently considered to be the fastest-growing area within the translation sector (Lockwood, 1999). Web localization means that the given site is provided in a specified language so that users can read text and navigate in their own language when they access the localized site. In other words, a localized Web site retains the same functionality as the original site. However, Web localization involves more than a straight translation of text. Cheng (2000:30–33) divides the process into three separate aspects: (1) front-end (what the user sees), including translation and cultural/marketing consideration; (2) back-end (technology behind the scenes), including engineering adjustments such as character encoding as well as maintenance, and (3) long-term developments to allow for evolution of functional features. Described as such, the task no longer sounds like the traditional translation process in which paper-based text is converted from the source into the target language. Converting a Web site into a given language version indeed is more akin to a software localization task than conventional translation work. Software localization involves engineering tasks as well as translation to enable the product to function in a given language environment. Web localization has made a significant impact on the translation process, as the Web as a communication medium has changed the nature of the Message in a number of ways.

Translating text for the Web is different from processing text intended for print-media for offline (as opposed to online) circulation. The following features may characterize the text used in a Web site:

(1)   the readership of the text is unspecified and can mean an extremely wide range of native speaker population;

(2)   the text will be read on screen rather than on paper, at least in the first instance;

(3)   the text may be read in any order, and therefore in different contexts, depending on which hyperlink the reader may follow;

(4)   the text is subject to much more frequent changes than is paper-based text;

(5)   the text may need to be 'adapted' to the target market readers, involving content changes; and

(6)   the text may contain multimedia components, such as audio and extensive graphics and icons, whose cultural appropriateness may need to be considered against the target-culture norms.

These features of online documents need to be taken into consideration by the translator. As such, translation of Web content requires that the translator understand the nature of the online medium. It will be difficult to obtain the best results from a translator who has never been online or surfed the Web. Immediate and wide exposure to native speaker readership means that the translation is required to be natural in the eyes of native Receivers. The computer screen as a reading medium means that screen aesthetics, such as font size, color of the font and page breaks in relation to screen size, need to be considered by somebody along the chain of production, if not by the translator. Also, lengthy sentences and long paragraphs are generally not welcome and the fact that the text may be accessed from different links means that readers may have a different context in which the text is read. Depending on the type of service or product for which the text is used and also depending on a target market, not only text but also non-textual visual elements may also require changes. This adjustment may be carried out upstream as part of the internationalization process (see Chapters 2 and 5) by the client before the text comes to the translator, but may often fall onto the translator's shoulders. Web text may also contain audio (speech) files, which need to be converted into the target language.

A full-scale Web localization, including site maintenance, is an expensive exercise. Updating Web site content every few hours in ten language versions is no easy feat, and those who localize their site are better advised to have an overall globalization strategy in place (see Chapter 5) to keep the exercise at a manageable level.

Interactive translation on the Web

The fact that not all Web sites are localized has, in turn, created an opportunity to fill in the need for interactive translation of Web sites by use of computer-based translation systems or MT. This kind of application, commonly known as WebMT, is specifically designed to allow Web navigation in a given language in near real-time. Quality of MT outputs is variable, depending on the type of the input text, but generally it is neither of publication-quality nor always reliable. Similar applications are being made on a number of search engines with which search results can be immediately linked to a translation engine (Chapter 3 discusses language-engineering solutions in more detail). In both these cases, the translation results seem to be typically used for information-only purposes. The characteristics of the needs for this type of language support are the speed and the convenience where the user does not have to leave the site to have the information translated. The pricing factor is also undoubtedly important: most of the MT-based services linked to search engines are provided free while some WebMT software is bundled with new computer purchases or sold at a very low price.

Table 1.2 summarizes language support that has emerged for the purpose of assisting global communication on the Web.

The task of Web localization is essentially asynchronous, no matter how short the deadline may be. However, once users start navigating the Web, they are free to choose where to go, making translation requirements dependent on the path they happen to choose. In addition to presenting information in an essentially asynchronous manner, the Web is also embracing CMC modes such as e-mail, text chat and more recently voice chat. As e-commerce matures, these modes will be integrated into customer interface functionality with suitable language support. Although e-mail is in itself an asynchronous mode of communication, the delay in response can be a cause for annoyance from the customer's viewpoint and can easily put them off. For this reason, translation of e-mail messages should ideally take place in near real-time. By comparison, text chat is a synchronous mode of communication in which participating parties type text interactively to communicate in real-time, and necessitates interactive language support as in the case of voice-based chat applications.

The term 'transterpreting' coined by Ashworth (1997) to describe what is needed to assist inter-lingual text chat suggests that language support for this mode of communication is a hybrid that involves translating text but doing it synchronously, as in interpreting. Furthermore, the choice of words used in chat text tends to be more akin to spoken language, making the text sometimes look like a transcript of speech. In this sense,

Table 1.2 Language support for globalizing communication on the Web

Types of language support needed for Web functionalities	*Description*
Web localization	This process allows a specific Web site to be viewed and navigated in a given language. It may involve some adjustments in terms of content and package such as visual design, depending on the target market and the strategy taken by the site provider.
Web navigation	This is a niche market currently served exclusively by MT systems. WebMT facilitates a user who does not understand the language used in a given web site by producing real-time translations on the fly.
Web search	Search engines are indispensable for finding information on the Web and therefore integrated translation solutions are sought. Some search portals themselves are localized into various language versions, while others are linked to a translation engine using an MT system whereby the user needs only to click the translation button. This area is also exclusively serviced by MT rather than its human counterparts.

transterpreting requires familiarity with the spoken form of language, in which the conventional translator may not always be well versed. A type of virtual meeting called computer conferencing uses text chat and also increasingly voice as the quality of the latter application improves. This will mean that language support needs to cater to both spoken and written forms of communication in synchronous mode. We will elaborate on transterpreting in Chapter 4.

Table 1.3 summarizes communication modes on the Web. and how they may become subject to TMC.

As illustrated by the birth of localization, which is clearly anomalous in relation to traditional forms of translation, the new communication environments suggest the need for new types of language support. The following section highlights how the language industry has responded so far to the emerging needs.

Table 1.3 CMC on the Web and TMC

Web communication modes	TMC
E-mail	E-mail is used for communication between individuals (one to one) or for posting messages to forum subscribers (one to many). Although e-mail itself is in asynchronous mode, its translation needs can be in near real-time when the recipient wishes to know the content of the foreign language message immediately or the sender of a message wishes to turn it into an appropriate language quickly before dispatching. CompuServe was the first to implement an MT-based service for a forum to allow for people with different mother tongues to exchange messages via e-mail.
Text-based chat	Text-based chat takes place in an interactive mode via typed text on computer screen. For this to take place between speakers of different languages, translation has to be provided interactively via typed text.
Voice-based chat	Chat using voice on the Internet is currently inferior in quality to the standard phone. However, it allows users to also use text chat functions concurrently with voice. In order for this mode of communication to be facilitated by interpreters, it is necessary for them to deal with both voice and text without seeing either of the speakers unless an image channel is also used.

Evolution of New Language Support

We will outline two particular developments during the 1990s that can be seen as precursors to a new generation of language support.

Rise of the localization industry

During the 1990s the localization business has grown rapidly to form an international industry. The need for localization reflected the increasing globalization process that was fuelled by the advancement of IT and the Internet in particular. The computer software localization business was first developed in the mid-1980s in response to the computer industry's need to increase its worldwide presence by making its products available in the given language of, and employing other relevant conventions used in, target markets (Jeanty, 1997). Reflecting the continuing globalization process, the boundary of the localization business has further extended into fields other than computer software, such as medical equipment, componentware, multimedia products and communications (Fry, 1998). The latest addition to the list is the Web, and this is becoming a significant area of work for localizers, as discussed above. Localization has come to mean rather comprehensive adaptation of the Message into the Receiver's environment in terms of both language and cultural context. In particular, the use of the electronic medium has come to mean that the translation process has become sufficiently invasive as to also affect the packaging in which the text is couched, whereas conventional translation tended to be a conversion of the content (i.e. text) alone. For example, compare the process involved in producing a Japanese version of Windows 98 and that of translating a paper-based manufacturing manual for circulation in print-based media. For the latter, the packaging aspect that may have been involved in the translation process is largely limited to desktop publishing (DTP), whereas the former requires engineering inputs to re-create the product for the Receiver's computing environment.

During the 1980s the translation industry started to expand beyond merely translating text to touch on packaging of the Message as in the case of DTP, whereby providing fonts and layout formatting of documents appropriate for the given language. However, software localization involves much more invasive processing of the packaging to embed the text in the digital environment, requiring engineering work such as adjusting character encoding. As such, the task is viewed as a much more value-added service, and accordingly is more closely associated with the end product, thus justifying a higher reward than the traditional paper-based translation product.

Given that the text subject to localization tends primarily to be embedded in a digital medium such as computer software or a Web site, the localization task is extremely IT-oriented to the extent that the production process itself involves the extensive use of IT. In this way, the localization industry has introduced a number of new elements to the conventional translation service, such as:

(1) Increased apparent added value to finished products;
(2) Started to streamline and quantify the translation process in terms of production and quality control;
(3) Introduced a new business model to the translation operation; and
(4) Contributed to awareness that translation is a critical ingredient for globalization.

Conventionally, exported goods have often been accompanied by some kind of translated documentation. Although such documentation was considered indispensable, the concrete value the translation may have added to the product was not readily measurable. With the maturing process of localization, the contribution made by localization to the sales revenue of the given products is becoming increasingly measurable. For example, in the 1998 financial year in excess of 60% of Microsoft's overall revenues were earned from markets outside of the USA (Brooks, 2000), illustrating a clear financial contribution of localization. In this sense, the localization industry has considerably raised the profile of the translation sector, as it was more readily able to demonstrate in a tangible manner the added value created by localization of which translation still is a significant part.

From the production side, however, localization has necessitated a more systematic and business-oriented approach than the conventional translation operation. This was necessary in order to deal with generally large-scale projects, involving co-ordination between localization engineers, translators and software publishers (clients). This has meant the need for project management as time-to-market is critically important for the release of software products. The deadline has always been the issue in the commercial translation sector, with the language service provider considering it too short and the client regarding it as far too long. The situation is no better with localization, as the release date is of extreme importance, particularly in the case of simultaneous shipment (simship) involving a number of language versions. This in turn made it necessary to apply a much more streamlined business model than the traditional translation operator would have ever applied. Project management and the control of the whole production process as well as quality management, have become necessary in many cases.

The localization industry has provided the example of language support as a significant leverage for globalization of business and now the new needs of e-commerce players to overcome linguistic and cultural barriers in virtual global marketplace are beginning to be recognized. The June 2000 Forrester Research report (Schmitt, 2000) states that multilingual web sites are no longer an option for US firms but a global business imperative. Localization is continuing to grow with the demand from the e-commerce sector to localize Web sites, and seems well positioned to evolve into the next generation of language support to assist global communication in cyberspace.

Globalization of translation operations

While the localization sector has risen as a new profit center with highly value-added services, the translation industry itself has become a global operation that champions the telework mode. Translation has traditionally been carried out independently in relation to the location of the Sender or the Receiver, and the current availability of electronic networks has reinforced this, making it possible to deliver text immediately, not only nationally but also internationally. In this way, the translation market expanded from regional to national during the 1980s initially by the use of fax and since the mid-1990s has expanded into the global marketplace based on the Internet. Towards the end of the 90s a handful of multi-national translation/localization corporations appeared that have the resources to set up a physical presence in strategic markets, as well as Web-based access to their worldwide customers. These organizations take advantage of Internet and Intranet connections to reach appropriate resources for a given assignment so that a wide range of languages and subject areas can be handled. While these large companies may operate as MLVs (multiple language vendors), offering a one-stop-shop solution for localization and translation needs, small companies tend to provide specialized services as SLVs, vendors of a single language or a limited range of languages mostly with a physical office in a single location where they can meet clients face to face.

When e-commerce first emerged, the concept of distributed translation was put into practice in terms of back-end operations linking subcontracted translators. In time, opportunities have risen for small-to-medium operators to provide global services from a virtual location with a Web site. Furthermore, there arose increased opportunities for freelance translators who have access to the Internet as so-called 'e-agencies' who are language brokers operating on the Web (e.g. http://www.aquarius.net) as well as direct clients seeking jobs through translators' forum groups and bidding sites (e.g. http://www.elance.com). With the maturing e-commerce market, some translation operators are going global in fully-fledged 'e' mode. According to an industry observer, the translation sector is becoming recognized by venture capitalists as a potential investment (Fry, 2000). An increasing number of these organizations are now developing into globalization service firms by offering a wide range of language support.

As e-commerce matures, needs for language support could grow exponentially. These newly developing needs are leading to the emergence of new types of language support that differ from conventional Translation in a number of ways. The following section illustrates the emerging characteristics of new language support, which we call *teletranslation* and *teleinterpretation*.

Emerging Needs for Teletranslation and Teleinterpretation

We will call the new language support teletranslation and teleinterpretation to distinguish them from conventional Translation. From the above discussion and also building on key requirements outlined by Fry (2000), we consider the following factors as critical for teletranslation and teleinterpretation to serve TMC on the Internet. Some of these issues are revisited in Chapter 7.

Critical factors

Speed

As the printing process is replaced by digital publishing on the Internet, the time lag between authoring of the source document and distribution has been considerably reduced. For example, any document produced on the computer can immediately be published on the Net by adding HTML tags. This will mean that translation is likely to come under increasing pressure to take less time, in some cases ideally no time. In the information society, the value of information diminishes in proportion to the age of the information. For some cases, if the time lag between authoring and translation exceeds a certain threshold, the information is no longer valid or needed. In this way, the timing factor is becoming ever more critical. The time pressure also comes from new modes of communication, such as text or voice chat, which are interactive and require synchronous language support as provided by interpreting services but without having face-to-face interactions.

Digital content

As the Internet is couched in the digital environment, Translation is now required to fit into packaging requirements arising from the new media. These may include design inputs for a Web site to ensure that non-textual components are also suitable for the target market. This, in turn, requires an understanding of digital media which we call digital literacy and also the use of certain IT tools. These issues are addressed in Chapters 2 and 3.

IT-device friendly

The Internet is currently being integrated into wireless communication via mobile phones so that people can access the Internet regardless of their location. As a result, many Internet services are beginning to make their access possible from mobile communications devices. WAP (wireless application protocol) and i-mode (NTT DoCoMo's Internet service over mobile phones) are currently the two major standards used to allow mobile Internet access (see Chapter 4). Language support is thus required to move together with such developments.

Another implication of the use of portable devices is that they make increasingly possible individual interactions between speakers of different languages, i.e. one-to-one translation becomes necessary perhaps in a great range of language combinations. The context in which TMC occurs at the moment is mostly one-to-many (one Sender to many Receivers). E-mail and communication by portable devices (mainly one-to-one) create problems now resolved primarily by MT and MI (machine interpretation), with their known limitations. What will be the implications of the need for high quality TMC via such portable devices?

Quality

An electronic medium such as the Internet often embraces a much wider reader population than printed media. For example, a localized Web page may be read by any of the online population who understands that particular language. This exposure will demand high quality translation, particularly in the context of e-commerce as potential customers can be repulsed by awkward translations. Quality will encompass the functionality of documentation and Web site design, including its hyperlink structures, use of graphics and the availability of synchronous and asynchronous modes of communication such as chat and e-mail. Furthermore, as is demonstrated by the localization industry, as translation becomes embedded in a given product, scalable quality measurements for translation will become increasingly important.

Pricing

The price factor is being affected by the whole dynamics of the Internet, which provides a lot of free information and utilities. Free translation services are now available with many search engine portals. This makes human-based language support seem extremely expensive and not suitable for the purpose of quick information sifting where much of the translation is disposed of almost immediately. This suggests that a new pricing method may be required.

Mixed modality of text and voice

As the Web incorporates both synchronous and asynchronous modes of communication seamlessly, there will be a need for both translation and interpretation to be available, and in some cases a hybrid mode such as transterpreting.

Value-addedness

What the localization industry has achieved is to tangibly demonstrate value-addedness by the use of language support. Furthermore, the value-added elements are increasingly linked to the integration of language support into digital media, involving engineering work. In other words, providing as an end product a translation of a paper copy of text for subsequent Web publication will no longer be perceived as a value-added service. The translated text needs to be embedded within the given medium in an elegant manner from the context of the Receiver's linguistic and cultural conditions. This necessitates the integration of engineering inputs into the conventional translation task.

Comprehensive globalization service

As the globalization process accelerates on the electronic communications infrastructure, it is becoming increasingly necessary to consider Translation as an integral part of globalization. By comparison, Translation has traditionally tended to be treated as an afterthought and has been considered separately from an organization's globalization strategies. Many early-adapters of Internet-based globalization are now recognizing that language and culture are an integral part of globalization and, as a result, they are seeking a service provider that can offer comprehensive support for their globalization on the Internet.

In this chapter we have discussed our approach based on Translation as communication and also TMC as the framework for our analysis. We have also surveyed the changes to Translation that are taking place, and outlined the requirements for language support to serve the need arising from the Internet. In the next chapter we will attempt to further highlight the new emerging context for teletranslation and teleinterpretation.

Topics for Further Research or Discussion

(1) If you are seeking language support to go global on the Internet, how would you go about finding it, and how would you describe your user specifications to the service providers?

(2) If you are a conventional translation service provider who wants to take advantage of the opportunities arising from the Internet, what are the major changes that you need to make?

Notes

1. For a discussion of 'objectivist' vs. 'constructivist' perceptions of reality, see the discussion in Kiraly (2000a), Chapter 2, pp. 34ff.

Chapter 2
Redefining Context for
Teletranslation and Teleinterpretation

In this chapter, we will examine the impact the Internet has had on translators, and its potential impact on interpreters. We will go beyond the most immediate concerns of e-business communication to include the set of possible ways of communicating through Translation that the Internet now affords. In doing so, we will explore new contexts for teletranslation and teleinterpretation, and define Translation as a communication system.

The Translator's New Workplace

The major defining events of the 'new workplace' are the computer and the Internet. Translators have been using computers in place of the typewriter since the mid-1980s. Much of the time they have used the computer for word processing and desktop publishing (DTP), i.e. to produce documents for distribution as 'physical' documents on paper. They have not been involved in the creation of Web pages or the translation of software now known as localization. They have used the Internet to send and receive documents, but not to create documents directly on the Internet. Interestingly, those who began with the IBM in the days of the original IBM PC, WordStar and WordPerfect, are somewhat familiar with the kinds of coding that are used to format Web documents (for example, in WordStar, ^psxxx^ps is used for 'underline xxx'). To compose any text with formatting such as italics, underline, bold, and the like, required knowledge of the formatting commands.

Translators who have been using the computer for more than 15 years, especially the IBM compatibles, have some familiarity with this kind of coding. The individuals at greatest disadvantage are those who are familiar only with the graphical, WYSIWYG (What You See Is What You Get) interface, but not with coding and manipulation of input. By now, translators have developed computer literacy to a large degree, some information literacy, and perhaps, the ability to work with Web pages. Some have become specialists in localization, who must be familiar with HTML, Java script, XML, and some computer languages such as C++ and/or Java – a

23

sea change from someone who does DTP or simply word processing. In most cases, the translator today supports both the production of text on paper and the electronic medium.

The Internet serves as a primary medium for a wide range of communications, from e-mail to voice chats to online learning, to virtual reality. The translator on a daily basis is now engaged in both 'atomic' media and 'digital' media. In atomic-mediated communication, the primary instrument of translation has been the typewriter and the production of paper documents. Although the computer has replaced the typewriter for the most part, the source and target texts are on paper. In digital communication, the primary instrument of communication is a digital device, be it a computer or digital phone, and a document that is produced is also digital, whether a newsletter, multimedia, software localized in another language, or Web page. The Internet, of course, serves as a vehicle for the distribution of documents that may ultimately end up in 'atomic' form if the Receiver prints out the document, but it also serves as a communication vehicle in its own right. When the Internet starts to include voice-communications as in the case of Internet phone, voice chat or voice messaging, there will be a need for voice-based language facilitation as well.

We will attempt to redefine the translator's workspace first in terms of its wider context. The change taking place can be illustrated in terms of the domain of conventional Translation and that of emerging teletranslation and teleinterpretation (see Figure 2.1). With the former, the predominant communication environment is analog/atomic, where translators deal mainly with text in print-media that are distributed by the physical transportation system, and interpreters operate mainly in face-to-face mode. By comparison, with teletranslation and teleinterpretation, translators cater mainly to digital contents, which are produced and distributed in digital media while interpreters carry out remote interpreting in virtual environments. We may illustrate the redefinition of the translator's workspace as shown in Figure 2.1, where the framework based on TMC becomes more applicable as we move to teletranslation and teleinterpretation.

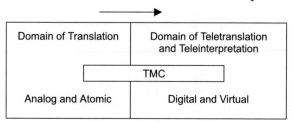

Figure 2.1   Redefinition of the Translator's workspace

Currently we are in a transitional phase sitting somewhere between the worlds of the analog/atomic and the digital/virtual. Advancements of communication technologies will mean increased interactions via the digital/virtual world, but this will never eliminate analog/atomic communications. So, the need for the conventional Translation will never disappear. At the same time, the Translator's workplace will need to be designed to cater to the digital/virtual world, as an increasing proportion of TMC will take place in such environments. The real distinction between TMC in the analog world and that in the digital and virtual world will be made when multimodal communication at a distance becomes the norm where people interact in tele-presence, as if in face-to-face situations, in a virtual communication space (see Chapter 10). Until then, the change will be gradual, whereby our dominant communications environment moves from atomic to the seamless integration of the virtual into the atomic. In this context, understanding of TMC will increasingly demand digital literacy. This encompasses the understanding of digital media and the nature of the Messages created and distributed in the digital environment.

We have discussed how the Internet has already affected the world of translation, for example, with such needs as Web localization. Web documents provide a good example to illustrate how the Message subject to Translation is changing. Figure 2.2 illustrates how digital content, such as Web documents, goes through its lifecycle. This is what we call the 'digital content lifecycle' based on the InfoCycle by Lockwood (1998).

Figure 2.2 shows key nodes involved in the lifecycle of digital content. It starts from authoring of text, which may include multimedia elements, followed by distribution. The user of such an information service accesses it via some kind of IT device and understands the content before taking some sort of action based upon the information. The information provider will use feedback from the customers to revise and update the content. Within this cycle, language support may be required at almost any point. For example, localization is typically applied after authoring and before distribution, whereas WebMT may be used to translate the specified site on the fly during the comprehension stage.

In such an environment, the need to go into a non-digital 'atomic' environment at any point tends to mean a disruption to the cycle. For example, a person wishing to have search engine results translated would ideally have a translation service on the screen where the search results are displayed. It would be impractical if the results had to be printed out and faxed to the Translator to receive a translation a few hours later. In this case, the Translation function would be incompatible with the seamless digital environment and the particular need. For this reason, many search engines are now

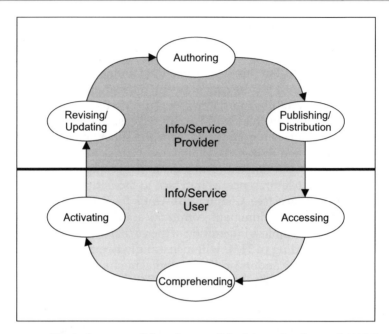

Figure 2.2 Digital content lifecycle, modified from Lockwood (1998)

offering a built-in MT-based service within a given search result that provides a seamless Translation function adequate at least for information sifting purposes.

In this way, the future Translator's workspace will have to be integrated into the information/communication system used by the Sender or/and the Receiver of the Message. In particular, such connectivity is essential for synchronous language support that will likely involve both text and speech via a range of communication devices. For example, developments of wireless communication such as mobile phones and other digital devices will need to be taken into consideration. It is likely that cyberspace will become the Translator's workspace in which an increasing proportion of translation and interpretation work will take place.

In sum, CMC in general succeeds to the extent that people embrace it and modify their own earlier assumptions (based on conventional patterns of communication) about how to communicate, and discover new ways and tools for communication that the Internet and telecommunications devices have the potential to provide. Once these tools are discovered, others accept and use them, thereby enriching, modifying, and newly defining Internet-based CMC. This also involves a complex process of cultural adaptation by different countries, which adapt new ways and technologies to their own cultural contexts (see Chapter 5). By implication, this serves to define and refine the ways in which TMC can operate (as long as participants are willing to accept them). TMC, therefore, like practically everything else that involves the Internet and telecommunications, continuously evolves and must adapt to new channels and modalities of communication. In the following section, we will further elaborate on digital literacy by focusing on Translation and Translator requirements.

Translation Competence and Translator Competence

Translation theorists often discuss translator competence (e.g. Bell, 1991; Wilss, 1996) in order to address knowledge and skills required for translators. With the significant changes currently taking place in communications environments, however, it is increasingly important to consider what is required of *translation* as an end product in addition to that of translators. Such views are supported by Sager (1993: 211) who stresses the role of Translation: 'as a commissioned task, which starts with a need for communication and ends with a finished product.' It is therefore useful to think about the requirements of Translation in terms of 'translation competence' and 'translator competence' as distinguished by Kiraly (2000a). The former refers primarily to the competence to produce acceptable translations, however one might define 'acceptable.' The latter term refers to the skills and knowledge a translator needs in addition to translation competence. One can argue that the nature of electronic documents has an influence on both translation competence and translator competence.

Translation competence

Electronic texts,[1] including audio and video communication, have characteristics not found in face-to-face or printed communication. The telephone is an obvious case of 'faceless voice communication,' in which all non-verbal paralanguage except modulation of the voice is absent. The interpretation of telephone conversations requires skills in rendering such messages in a manner appropriate to the context. In current videoconferencing technology, eye contact is not possible, although many visual cues will be present. Unlike face-to-face communication, however, there is no counterpart to other modalities such as proxemics.

Let us review some other features of Internet communication that may have an impact on translation competence. Here, we are examining TMC from a broader perspective than the newly established communications patterns that have emerged with the arrival of e-commerce (e.g. Collot & Bellmore, 1996). We limit our discussion here only to outline major characteristics of some of the new modes of communication in relation to translation competence, since more thorough treatment of CMC modes is given in Chapter 4.

Text chat

Text chat may take place in a casual anonymous setting or in more controlled business or instructional environments. In either case, turn-taking cues are normally absent, unless special protocols are set up, which often require a designated person to monitor the interaction, and such protocols depend on a willingness or awareness of the participants to use them. Even in a chat between two people, turn signals are not obvious, since back channeling, which is prevalent in face-to-face communication, is not automatically available.

Voice chat

We have extensively used this mode of communication during our experiment with a pilot teletranslation and teleinterpretation course (see Chapter 8). On the basis of our experience combined with our trials with other similar platforms, we have found the following:

As in text chat, turn taking is still a problem, since signals are needed to indicate

- the desire to speak;
- back-channeling (in particular, the speaker needs to be aware of back channeling in order to know that he is getting the message across);
- turn-taking signals. However, this issue is being recognized, as in the case with a commercial voice platform Paltalk™, which uses a raised hand icon to signal the wish to speak, and a microphone icon to indicate who is speaking (see Figure 8.2);
- the effects of half duplex. Most voice chat programs use 'push to talk' e.g. 'hold down the Ctrl key to speak' making back channeling and interruption difficult, if not impossible. These problems are compounded by inconsistent transmission quality of speech.

Hypertext

We have discussed specific features of Web documents in Chapter 1. The following underlines new elements pertinent to hypertext in light of translation competence. The impact of hypertext on the structure of discourse needs to be investigated before any definitive statements can be made. However, we observe the following:

- text is not linear. If choices exist within a single document to view related parts by means of links, cohesive devices may differ from those used in conventional documents that follow a linear sequence;
- in such situations, pronouns and anaphora may also be affected;
- in interactive linking, a destination could be sensitive to the link from which it was selected (in the case of more than one link in text A going to text B).

These new forms of discourse result in new language practices, some of which are evolving currently and may differ widely according to the cultures of the users. As an early adopter example, a French and English bilingual conference held in Canada in 1996 used text chat (Internet Relay Chat or IRC) as an official communication channel to link off-site participants to the on-site conferees in real-time with a special interpreting arrangement. We will elaborate on this new form of language facilitation in Chapter 4.

For some languages, the above new forms of communication may pose special problems or not be acceptable. In Chinese, for example, keyboard input is so slow that text chat is avoided by some. If speech recognition becomes sufficiently advanced, text chat in Chinese would become more feasible. Theoretically, the application of speech recognition is suited to a language such as Chinese, which distinguishes homonyms in terms of different tones when they are spoken if the technology is capable of detecting the gradation of these tones. This is a distinct advantage of the Chinese language over Japanese, for example, in which homophones can correspond to many different combinations of characters, depending on the intended meaning.

In other cases, a culture may not prefer the 'liberating' experience that online chat allows (Schrage, 1995). It may be important in that culture for participants to know who is speaking (chatting), and to identify themselves as speakers. The use of certain communication modes could thus cause a problem for intercultural communication. In particular, turn taking may pose special problems, not simply because of the technical design but because of cultural differences in terms of ease of speaking out when one does not know if it is one's turn. Such problems are reported in Palloff and Pratt (1999).

Translator competence

Teletranslators and teleinterpreters therefore need a wide range of knowledge and skills to be literate in the digital environment. In addition to translating or interpreting the conventional Message in the conventional mode, they will increasingly be involved in translating such digital contents as software, web pages, and multimedia.

Software localization

This requires both an understanding of the inner workings of the software being translated and an understanding of linguistic problems stemming from language differences in the given genre of software domain (e.g. games, general consumer products, business applications). These issues are dealt with in great detail in the text *A Practical Guide to Localization* (Esselink, 2000a), but do merit some treatment here. In order to localize a program, it is necessary to have access to the underlying code of that program, which is usually written in a language such as C++, Java, Visual Basic, and the like. Ideally, localization is a collaborative effort between the localizer and the publisher (in particular, the software engineer) who created the original software. The localizer translates the source language strings, compiles the program module, and views the results. Very often, problems arise based on language differences. The simplest problem is length of source vs. target language strings. For example, a button may have a short English label that would be much longer in the target language. Japanese translations of English text, for example, tend to be several-to-many characters longer than the English source. A formatted two-column list with word-wrap in English may, upon translation, result in awkward-looking target language formatting. Often the localizer (or engineer) must rewrite some of the source code to compensate for the differences.

Ideally, one designs software with localization in mind before committing it to code (see 'Internationalization' below). This is especially important with operating system software and the menus and other language features that need to be consistent across programs. A software developer for a program that runs under both Windows and Macintosh, for example, who plans to create foreign-language versions of the software, must conform strictly to the interfaces of the two operating systems and use consistent terms and commands.

Web localization

Similarly, the Web localizer needs experience working with Web languages, ranging from HTML to XML to JavaScript and Java. Tools exist to make localization of both software and Web pages more efficient and consistent (e.g. TRADOS, Deja Vu), as we discuss in the next chapter. However, these tools are often insufficient to handle the finer points of the encoding, making it necessary to tweak the code to create the desired result.

Internationalization

The translator will work with a source text that the Sender prepared to reach an audience beyond the Sender's native language. Sometimes, as a practice in technical writing (e.g. of operating manuals and the like), the writer/Sender follows guidelines to simplify a source text to make it as intelligible as possible to both native and non-native readers. This may simply be a matter of conforming to an in-house style sheet, or a more extensive effort to adopt a controlled language, which we discuss below. In Web design for globalization, Senders follow a similar practice both to ensure intelligibility and to facilitate translation. However, translators face the same problem in targeting a particular audience as they do in translating advertising copy: the necessity to customize the target documents for the culture of the Receiver. Internationalization can help in many cases, but the translator bears ultimate responsibility for the appropriate linguistic form of the target document.

Figure 2.3 shows this diagrammatically. In **1** 'afterthought translation' means that the source language text is not prepared with translation in mind. This may result in awkward translation for the target language Receiver in large parts resembling the source language (translatese). In **2** the Receiver is a speaker of the source language, so there is no translation required. In **3** the source language is modified by being internationalized, and is understandable both to a Receiver who speaks the source language and to a Receiver for whom it is a second language. In **4** the internationalized text is further

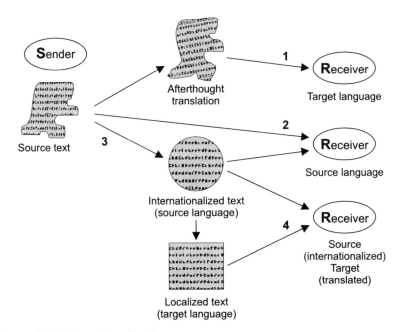

Figure 2.3 Internationalization process

localized to become intelligible to other Receivers, who do not know the source language. The internationalization process makes the Message more amenable to the subsequent translation into the Receiver's language. Note that the form of the Message changes, as represented by different shapes. The different shapes illustrate certain preferences by the culture of the target language. In this particular case, the culture of the target language prefers squares to circles.

Tools

Given the new type of tasks as described above, Translator competence also includes proficiency in using certain tools. Since the next chapter includes this topic, here we will mainly discuss the rationale for the use of such tools in relation to the nature of the Message. Dealing with digital content means that the Message is provided in a machine-readable form, which automatically facilitates the use of certain tools. MT is probably the best example, although it is hardly used as a regular 'tool' by most translation providers. Other tools include Translation Memory, terminology management systems, electronic dictionaries, and online databases, all of which work most efficiently with digital text. Otherwise the text needs to be retyped or to go through OCR (Optical Character Recognition), which is time-consuming and may introduce errors. Another important tool is management software of various kinds, such as workflow programs, including translation manager programs. These tools assist in organizing files, work procedures and flows.

In light of translation and translator competence requirements, we will attempt to redefine the new environment in which TMC will increasingly take place.

Redefining the Context

In exploring the new context of teletranslation and teleinterpretation, we return to our framework based on TMC, and consider our view of Translation as communication. We have argued that, as the infrastructure for communication changes, the Message changes and the mechanism of processing, storing and transmitting the Message changes. This is already amply demonstrated by today's CMC. We have also argued that TMC adds a special language facilitation dimension to CMC. A good example is search engines that have incorporated translation functions (see Chapter 3). As we move into the teletranslation and teleinterpretation domain with its dominant digital/virtual environments, it is useful to treat Translation as a communication system consisting of process, storage and transmission functions. Figure 2.4 shows a Translation Communication System with the underlying communication flow between the Sender (S) and the Receiver (R2) of the Message (M2) in the target language, as explained in Figure 1.1. The Translator carries out their function by applying their internal knowledge stored in their biological memories as well as in auxiliary memories such as dictionaries and databases in order to process (translate or interpret) the given Message (written or spoken), which is transmitted to the Receiver. For such a system to function, it also needs a control function, which takes in feedback and maintains the system as a whole. This basic concept is applicable to computer-based natural language processing systems such as Machine Translation (MT) and Machine Interpretation (MI) as we discuss in the next chapter.

Translation Communication System

The following outlines the key functions of the Translation Communication System envisaged for teletranslation and teleinterpretation in the predominantly digital environment. We will focus on new aspects emerging in each of the three primary functions.

Processing

One of the new requirements for the translator arising from the new environment is that of pre-processing issues. For example, text delivered in digital form means that appropriate software is needed to deal with varying formats in which the Message arrives. They may be HTML, RTF (rich text format), PDF (portable document format) as well as Microsoft Word documents that may contain JPEG pictures or RealAudio files. Today, many text editing products are available to allow the translator to be able to

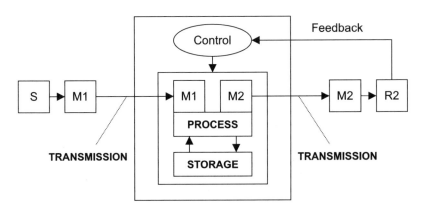

Figure 2.4 Translation Communication System

process text without being distracted by these formats (see Chapter 3). Other issues relating to pre-processing are internationalization and the use of controlled language. Computer-based translation systems have tended to require some kind of pre-editing to re-cast the source text to make it suitable for machine processing. The use of controlled language incorporates this process into authoring of the text, and is implemented primarily to allow for the subsequent use of MT systems on the text. The internationalization process aims to build flexibility into the product design to accommodate different language and cultural versions that may be developed. These pre-processing aspects can be considered as prominent changes occurring. We discuss the internationalization issue in some detail in Chapter 5.

Another issue highlighted by the Internet is that of multilingual text processing in terms of character encoding systems. In fact, they affect storage and transmission as well processing functions. While any alphabet-based European languages, including Greek and Cyrillic-based languages, can be represented using a standard one-byte (7 or 8 bit) character code per letter, languages that use a large number of character sets such as Chinese, Japanese and Korean (often abbreviated as CJK) clearly cannot be accommodated within the above scheme.

The ASCII (American Standard Code for Information Interchange) global standard for electronic encoding of characters defines a one-byte coding for upper and lower case Roman alphabet as well as Arabic numerals and symbols. The ASCII character set consists of 128 characters and is normally represented by seven bits. There are also nine extended ASCII character sets using eight-bit byte encoding which accommodate Arabic, Hebrew and Cyrillic languages (Lunde, 1993). However, these still do not provide enough space for CJK character sets. A resolution of the problem for multilingual text processing and communications over computer networks is being sought with Unicode, a 16-bit encoding framework. Unicode was designed to become the worldwide character-encoding standard although it has its drawbacks, for example, in terms of the CJK 'unification' issue and storage since all characters (including those conventionally represented in single-byte code) are double-byte. Even though conceptually this is a major step forward, the problems of encoding languages are by no means resolved. It is as much a political issue, as it is a logical, technical one (see Chapter 5). As long as countries do not subscribe to the use of a uniform standard of encoding, there will be a constant need for troubleshooting. And yet, this is a minimum infrastructure needed to realize multilingual language support.

Storage

The most prominent recent change in the storage function for the translator is the concept of Translation Memory (TM), which allows the recycling of previous translations. We will limit the discussion on TM here to a minimum, as Chapter 3 deals with the topic. TM systems in effect bring storage and processing functions closer together. For example, a TM system will show parts of the text that need to be freshly translated, whereas the segments of text that appeared before are marked so that the translator can simply replace them with the existing translations (the translator is normally given a chance to review if the available translation is suitable). Another prominent change in terms of storage is the use of distributed database functions such as the Internet on which the translator is able to carry out various terminology or parallel text searches. Here the Internet functions as a gigantic corpus in a wide range of languages.

By comparison, although interpreters also benefit from the Internet as a text and terminology database prior to the actual interpreting performance, they are mainly reliant on their biological memories once the session starts in real-time. However, new storage functions appearing on some CMC modes may have an implication for teleinterpretation. For example, with certain chat sessions the text or speech exchanged can be recorded for a subsequent retrieval. Such capabilities point to a new possibility of speech manipulation and storage. Currently the corpus-based approach to natural language processing seems popular with such applications as example-based machine translations (EBMTs) and translation memories. However, these databases contain only written words. In future, the opportunity may arise to build a large speech-based corpus with a possible implication for interpretation memory as well as for Machine Interpretation (MI).

Transmission

Today's translation operations commonly use e-mail to send and receive the text. This means that the text is received in machine-readable form ready for further computer processing. The digital transmission environment also permits multimedia contents. Another significant development in terms of transmission function is the use of wireless devices such as mobile phone and various PDAs (Personal Digital Assistants). The implication of these developments for a Translation system is a greater mobility of teletranslators and teleinterpreters, who do not have to be bound to their computers in the office or conference center. However, for teleinterpretation to take place, a certain speech transmission quality has to be obtained, as we discuss in Chapter 7.

In a later chapter, we will touch on the possible changes to teletranslation and teleinterpretation when the infrastructure begins to allow three-dimensional virtual reality to be freely transmitted between the Sender and the Receiver. The shift from paper to screen to immersive virtual reality interactions is a significant transformation of the communication media and TMC, particularly in relation to interpreting, which has previously been reliant on the 'atomic' presence of communicating parties.

In this chapter we have shown in broad brush the emerging context in which translators and interpreters need to operate in the shift to tele-translation and teleinterpretation. Our aim has been to give a taste of the changes that are taking place right now, and to link those to further trans-formation into future developments. In one sense, the digital environment begs for language solutions based on natural language processing – with its speed and streamlined processing of text and speech. In particular, synchronous language support needs have already created new computer-based applications. The next chapter deals with the progress with language engineering, which is not only producing MTs but is also producing an array of useful tools to assist the human translation process.

Topics for Further Research or Discussion

(1) Based on your own experience, how has the nature of the tasks of the translator changed over the past decade?

(2) If you are a translator or a translation service provider, what do you think is the ideal translation communication system, which caters to the emerging needs arising from the Internet?

Note

1. We use the term 'text' as defined by Halliday (1989), i.e. as any piece of language, whether in spoken or written form.

Chapter 3
Language Engineering and the Internet

The recent growth of the Internet has highlighted the use of computer-based language solutions to enable seamless multilingual support in cyberspace. For example, most major search engines have now incorporated free real-time translation services based on Machine Translation (MT). Furthermore, the human translation process is facilitated by more and more sophisticated tools that are designed to enhance productivity as well as quality. In this way, language engineering will increasingly play a significant role in language support. In this chapter, we will consider this topic from the interest of four main parties who have different stakes in the development of language engineering. We will also describe new specialists emerging from language engineering in response to the demand.

Overview: Translation and Technology

Technology impacts translation in several ways: it can provide new tools to support the translation process, and it forms the basis for the birth of new literacies. These new literacies involve a shift in ways of communicating. New tools refer to (1) tools that make translation more efficient and respond to the needs that emerge from new literacies, and (2) tools needed to support the new forms of communication, especially those brought about by information and telecommunications technologies. By 'new literacies' we refer in particular to the shift from exclusive reliance on the printed word and paper media and on analog media such as radio and television, to the digital age, in which 'documents' may appear only in electronic form and include graphics, animation, voice and video as well as text. Even the word processor, not to mention the typewriter, may no longer be an adequate tool to support translation efforts in these new media.

We will examine these areas and place them in two major time frames: *past* and *non-past*. While it is true that most translators will continue to find traditional, conventional work, there has been a surge of demand for translators and interpreters literate in information technology (IT), who must possess new knowledge and skills in order to work with that technology.

We are thus concerned about time, because translation is moving rapidly into these new areas of multilingual support for the communication efforts of businesses and other institutions. The rapid pace at which startup companies must work in order to make a profit and satisfy their investors, especially in the areas of technology and telecommunications, is reflected also in the communication needs of these companies in dealing with countries where other languages are spoken. In their attempt to remain on the leading edge, they wish to utilize the new technologies to the fullest.

The typewriter is almost obsolete as a device to produce translated documents. It belongs to the past. The 'non-past' includes the obsolescent, the current, the new innovations, and the future over the horizon. The dedicated word processor belongs to the obsolescent categories. Word processing programs and other office software such as Microsoft Office are 'current.' New innovations include – especially for the translator – voice-recognition software that currently has a much higher accuracy rate than even one year ago. Over-the-horizon developments would include the use of hand-held devices with large memories and storage, adequate methods of displaying information, and excellent voice recognition, so that translators would not even need a desk to work from if they chose not to do so. And an ultimate goal of technology in the context of Translation is extensive automation as has been pursued by MT and Machine Interpretation (MI) research and development. The following comments on recent developments of MT, particularly on the Internet.

Machine translation (MT)

As the Internet incorporates synchronous communication via text and voice, the need for interactive language support is on the increase. This is where MT appears to excel, while human-based translation is perceived to be too slow and expensive. When MT research first started more than half a century ago, mainly driven by the need for intelligence gathering, today's communication context was clearly not on the minds of researchers and developers. As many involved in MT today comment (see Nishigaki, 1999; Tanaka, 1999), the Internet has brought about fresh rationale for language engineering in general and MT in particular. MT at the present time has a primary function of providing the gist of a document. It is unsuited to providing any kind of 'official' translation without human intervention. Nevertheless, in some cases MT can be fairly accurate particularly between close languages, such as Spanish and Portuguese, Swedish and Danish, French and Italian, and so on. However, even if the languages are close to each other, the subject matter of the document may make MT ineffective.

With online MT programs such as Amikai (http://www.amikai.com) or Alis (http://www.alis.com), one can copy a portion of text and paste it into the program directly on screen to receive a translation. Various programs on the Web provide MT, but they each offer a different range of language combinations. Alis, for example, does not currently translate from Japanese, although it does provide translation into that language. It is instructive to experiment with online MT programs to see what kind of output they produce. One of the authors has experimented with Amikai taking an English sentence, translating it into Portuguese or French, and then translating it back into English from one of those languages. Sometimes the result is similar and intelligible. At other times, the result is quite meaningless. It seems that certain types of texts lend themselves rather well to MT. More success was achieved by translating straight narrative or description than with other types of texts such as arguments or highly idiomatic documents. Another experiment with a Japanese/English online MT at http://www.excite.co.jp/world/text revealed that, merely by shortening the length of input sentence (in Japanese), the result improved markedly.

MT has value in assisting the user of the Web to search for documents on a particular topic in foreign languages and for gisting the meaning of documents, including Web pages. The search engine AltaVista allows the user to translate the search input and to translate the foreign language hits that the engine finds, using BabelFish, one of several translation engines on the Web designed for this purpose. First one goes to the AltaVista site and enters an (English) search string, then one selects the language that one wishes to find the references for. For example, one enters 'bioterrorism,' and selects Japanese as the language to search for references. Once the engine conducts the search, one can request an MT translation of the pages found, into English, for example. BabelFish will provide a translation of the entire text, including captions and table contents. The intelligibility of the translation will depend on the nature of the source text.

The evolution of MT from expensive and exclusive mainframe systems through much cheaper PC-based programs down to publicly available free online programs has made automatic language support something of a utility. In a similar way Hutchins (1999), an MT expert, predicts that in future word processing programs will likely incorporate MT functions. We will later briefly revisit MT as a translator's tool.

Language Engineering

The term 'language engineering' is explained by the European Commission as follows: 'language engineering applies knowledge of language to the development of computer systems that can recognize, understand, interpret, and generate human language in all its forms' ('The Doctor is in,' 1998). In this section, we view the language engineering problem from four perspectives: the enterprise that seeks engineering solutions, the language engineer, the translator and the teacher of Translation. We would also like to add another type of engineer, the 'translation engineer,' who is directly involved in TMC as well as language engineering.

The enterprise

With the advent of the Internet, enterprises have sought to use engineering to solve most of their problems. Engineering solutions are designed for efficiency, economy and, in business, rapid completion of a project or delivery of a product. While this may be true for the Internet environment, when it comes to human interaction and the need to understand language, the assumptions made by engineers can go only so far. This has been the case in the past with MT, where electrical engineers often attempted to create programs for MT on the basis of their knowledge of computers, but not necessarily of linguistics or language. The enterprise, of course, is faced with the need for accurate, low cost, and rapid delivery of an increasing volume of translation. The computer appears to be the rational solution to all of these problems. Unfortunately many of the issues arising in MT and other uses of technology to solve language problems stem from the lack of knowledge and expertise in the field of linguistics or translation. One of the main features of human usage of natural language is that it always occurs in context and its meaning is indeterminate without the context (Kay *et al.*, 1994). This very adaptability of natural language makes successful translation by MT extremely difficult. Melby (1995) also points to the fact that there is always a human motivation behind language use. This relates to the fact that language is situated and is never used in a vacuum. While these are helpful reminders to human translators, most current generation MT systems are unable to cope with this very nature of language use, which rarely allows a one-to-one match between two languages.

A practical example from experience of seeking an engineering solution to language problems is the case of a company that acquired an online dictionary and attempted to create a proof-of-concept catalog for an e-commerce marketing venture. The heading for the table of contents page in their catalog, which was in Japanese, (translated from English) contained the word *shisuu*. Apparently they looked up the word 'index' in a bilingual dictionary and selected the first entry in the dictionary. Unfortunately, the term that they selected is used in such contexts as '*index* of leading economic indicators,' but is not used in the sense of an index or table of contents of a document. Since they did not know the target language, they could not know the meaning of the term they selected, and, as a result, the reader would simply be confused by such terminology. Another, more serious problem from the same company, was the attempt to create bilingual glossaries of source documents by developing spreadsheets with single word entries. The idea was to create such a glossary to facilitate looking up words and possibly to automate part of the translation process on this basis. In so doing, they failed to realize that a word such as 'Visa,' which refers to a credit card in most of the contexts that they were dealing with, would be translated as 'permit to enter a country.' In both cases, the engineers in charge failed to recognize the importance of context in choosing the proper equivalent in the target language.

As can be seen, engineering solutions can best be carried out in consultation with people who are knowledgeable about cross-linguistic problems, the limitations of technology, and the prime importance of context in translation. An article in the LISA Newsletter (Homnack, 2000) criticizes companies for their over exuberance in seeking engineering solutions to their human problems. While solutions based on language engineering may look attractive from a short-term view, the enterprise that is considering applying such solutions must give careful consideration to the types of communications (Messages) that become subject to such solutions. The topic of the next chapter includes language management, which can also be considered as an engineering-oriented solution and yet incorporates much more long-term strategic thinking than the 'plug-and-play' approach demonstrated by some organizations seeking an indiscriminate instant solution.

The language engineer

Language engineers usually have a background in linguistics and computer science, including computational linguistics. They deal with such problems as the analysis of sentences and higher level discourse, the formulation of programs to translate from one language to another based on an analysis of both of them, the creation of dictionaries and glossaries, the creation of programs to summarize or create abstracts of documents, the creation of parallel texts between one language and its translation into another, and other issues that involve a knowledge of linguistics and the manipulation of language. The tasks often relate to the work traditionally carried out by lexicographers and terminologists, but using computers extensively as the main tool.

Language engineers are likely to run into several types of problems if they are not familiar with the languages being processed. This may happen even if they are generally aware of the nature of the languages they are dealing with. This is especially true in the case of orthographies that do not follow the typical Western pattern, i.e. alphabetic languages. A common problem facing companies who have hired language engineers is the realization, for example, that double-byte languages do not distinguish words by inserting blanks between them. In other words, a single paragraph consists of long strings of characters that may have punctuation marks such as periods and commas, but no visible distinction of word boundaries.

In most of the languages of the world, a word in a text is defined as a string of characters that is bounded on one or both sides by a blank space. This makes it very simple to create a word list in alphabetical order, and to create concordances of texts. It is a simple matter of separating the words, putting them in alphabetical order, counting them, and creating an index of each word to its context in the original text. It is quite a mechanical process. However, in the analysis of Japanese or Chinese, the only way to create a word list is through a lengthy process of matching each character in a text against a dictionary in order to determine how many characters in a string belong to a word. If the dictionary is not comprehensive, it may miss certain entries in the text. For example, consider what would happen in English if all of the words in a sentence were run together. The text would look something like this:

WhatwouldhappeninEnglishifallthewordsinasentencewereruntogether?

Because there are no spaces between the words, there is no convenient way to distinguish one word from another. Of course, the beginning of the line is capitalized, there's a question mark at the end, and proper nouns are capitalized. Aside from that, it is necessary to make a continuous series of matchings until a word is discovered in a dictionary and printed out into a list. This is exactly what happens when one attempts to create word lists or count words in double-byte languages.

Language engineers can provide input to other staff in resolving such problems as localization of a Web site, the extraction of text from graphics, creating algorithms for counting words, language recognition, and font problems. Typically, they are also involved in the development of translation memory systems, MT, the production of glossaries and dictionaries, the development of parallel texts, and associated lower-level problems in development of such tools. Since they also understand and may be able to utilize various programming languages, they can interact with software engineers in the development of foreign language Web pages and other types of documents.

The Translator

The primary problem, which is still quite common in the business community, is the naive belief that MT is an acceptable engineering solution for providing rapid, inexpensive, accurate translation of a source text that has been created for the benefit of speakers of the target language. In other words, the Sender believes that MT can replace the human translator in preparing a translation for the Receiver. This was pointed out above in reference to the problem with the word 'index.' One must always bear in mind the purpose of a given translation. Much of the time, for Internet surfers the purpose of the translation is merely to get the general idea of a foreign language document. In the case of intelligence work, however, the translation usually must be very accurate. In the case of routine correspondence, the gist of the document is often sufficient. Sometimes, a client may want to know something about the content of a foreign language document in order to decide whether or not to have it translated (by a human translator). On the other hand, when an enterprise wishes to present itself in an appropriate manner on the Web to people in foreign countries, it must use accurate, idiomatic language. For the latter purpose, it is essential to use a human translator who has an up-to-date, idiomatic, native knowledge of the target language and culture.

The translator, in turn, reaps the benefits of the work both of language engineers and of Internet engineers in general. This may include dictionary CD-ROMs, various types of word processing programs and desktop publishing (DTP) tools. Now they have software tools to help them resolve the basic issues in terminology search and acquire the necessary background information to provide appropriate translation in context, and translation memory for translating a large volume of frequently updated documents by recycling existing translations.

We will now look in turn at the tools that support Translation.

Machine translation (MT)

While translators in general find much fault with MT, there is a small group of translators who use it on a more regular basis. Sometimes a translator is able to produce a rough draft of a text by using the MT program and then edit it. For example, there is a patent translation company that extensively uses MT to provide a base translation on which human translators work. One of the authors has seen a reasonably successful first draft translation of a chapter of *Harry Potter* from English into French that was produced with the aid of an MT program. Another example is the case where translators use it to analyze the sentences of a source text by viewing the translated output. In this case, they are using a program that has highly accurate parsing algorithms. Even though the translation may be lexically incorrect, it may reveal the proper analysis of the structure of the source sentence.

MT and other types of support tools for translators generally depend on the word, not on the concept. However, in future it may become possible to search for meaning parallels rather than word parallels. In an article on 'Emerging technologies that will change the world' (Waldrop & Jensen, 2001), there is a discussion on natural language processing. For example, Microsoft has a new technology called 'MindNet' that is able to interpret a sentence such as 'please arrange for a meeting with John at 11:00,' as 'make an appointment with John at 11.' The ability of software to para-phrase a text indicates that it is sensitive to at least the lexical meaning of the source text and some of its pragmatic aspects. This could give a signifi-cant boost both to machine translation and to other types of processing and searching for text.[1]

Translation memory (TM)

Many translators have purchased TM systems at considerable expense in order to make it easier to carry out large projects. This may also have been in response to the pressure from certain clients who insist on the use of TM if the translator wants to win the contract. With the recent advent of application service providers (ASPs) that provide online support in the form of TM systems, extraction of text from HTML and XML and other code, glossaries and the like, translators may no longer need to go to the expense of purchasing such software. In exchange for such convenience, their work is provided by a specific translation service provider, and all output from the translators, including glossaries that they develop, become the property of the provider. The main (and great) convenience to the trans-lator is the ability to work online with a minimum of tools. On the negative side, such convenience may be offset in certain countries by the access fees that local telephone companies charge to go online.

TM systems are used primarily to facilitate the translation of a large volume of documents, especially new versions of old documents that (1) have already been translated and (2) share many identical or nearly-iden-tical sentences and terms. The previous source and target texts comprise a database that can be used to ensure consistency in the use of terminology, phraseology, style and other aspects of the translation task, without having to employ multiple editors to ensure consistency. A TM system contains an editable online glossary, a large database containing previous translations and source text of same, and text-alignment, which is a method for comparing a source sentence with a database in order to see whether or not that sentence has already been translated, or something very similar to the new source sentence is in the database. Some systems allow translators to select from a number of candidate phrases based on fuzzy logic.

Since TM is based on collections of parallel texts, which compare and match a source and target translation, it has the potential for creating very large, context-sensitive databases that can be of immense value to any translator, as long as these databases can be accessible. One of the primary problems confronting any translator is the use of language in context. For this reason, bilingual glossaries and dictionaries are usually very inadequate, especially if they contain only single-word definitions. For example, words such as modality, regime and system have many different translations in other languages, depending on the knowledge domain, and other types of context. In European languages, these words are 'false friends,' and must be treated with care. Given the presence of a large database of parallel texts, it should be possible to find appropriate equivalents for these terms by searching through texts in the same domain.

As natural language processing becomes increasingly sophisticated, it may become possible not only to search for equivalents of a given string of words, but also to find alternative equivalents as paraphrases of the source language, matched against texts in the target language. Significant business impact of TM systems is that the clients are becoming reluctant to pay twice for a sentence that has been translated before. This is likely to have a long-term implication for translation providers on their charging method as well as for the ownership of the content of TM systems.

Extraction tools

Extraction tools allow the translator to view a Web document without having to see the underlying HTML, XML or JavaScript code. Since the translators are able to see only the texts, they will not be confused by having to search through the code to find the source text that needs to be translated. Extraction tools are not normally provided as independent programs for downloading or purchase, but reside on the server of the translation service provider and must be used for the particular client.[2] Some recent versions of translation memory products have also incorporated such tools. A typical example of an extraction tool is the Passport program developed by Worldpoint. The translator can see the text of the source document surrounded by marks indicating the presence of underlying code. The translator selects the source text, and replaces it with the target language equivalent. It is then possible to view the translation to see whether or not the formatting is still intact. In the case of Passport, an editor edits the translation and the production department takes care of formatting problems.

Experience will show that having a stand-alone extraction tool on the desktop will normally be insufficient to provide a finished translation of a Web page because of problems with word length, wrapping of words at the end of lines, and other formatting issues.

The Internet as a resource

The Internet itself, especially Internet search engines, provides a valuable resource for resolving terminology problems. Search engines allow the translator to search according to various patterns: language, by country, and by domain. At the present time, translation from English into other languages is perhaps the most common type of translation being carried out on the Web. As a result, it is often possible to look up an English word or phrase and find the appropriate context and translation of the term in another language. Take, for example, the term 'wavelength division multiplexing,' or WDM. Since this term also has an acronym, it is rather simple to find foreign-language equivalents of this term by searching for the two terms, in English, restricted to the countries where the target language is spoken.

Another, rather typical example, is the need to find a set equivalent for a proper name or term. An example provided here is from one of the authors' own experience. The US federal government daily publishes translations of articles in the foreign press (newspapers, Web documents, and others) for consumers inside the government. In the area of science policy, these include articles that report on funding for scientific research, proposals before the Japanese Diet, science news events, and the like. Since searching a database can access the translated articles, obviously the translations must be consistent.

The problem is that often specific terms, and especially the names of organizations and events, are not translatable unless one knows exactly what the equivalents are in the two languages. For example, the term *Nichibei Houkatsu Keizai Kyougi*, literally 'Japan–US Comprehensive Economic Conference,' has the official translation of 'US–Japan Framework Talks on Bilateral Trade.' The original term for the event was probably the English term, while the Japanese version is an explanatory version of the English and is also the official Japanese translation. The consumer using the government database obviously will be searching for information about the 'framework talks,' not about a 'comprehensive economic conference.' It is often possible to look up either the original English term or the Japanese one and find the translation in the other language. This is quite similar to the problem of determining, or discovering, the proper English equivalents of the name of a foreign company. A company may create an English name for itself that is not a direct translation of the original native language name. For example, the Japanese organization *Kokusai Kouryuu Kikin*, which literally means 'International Exchange Foundation' is officially known in English as the 'Japan Foundation.'

Speech recognition[3]

Recently, speech recognition software has become sufficiently sophisticated that it can be used easily in place of typing at the keyboard. In fact, this chapter is being written primarily by using such software. Although the system is not entirely accurate, the number of edits that must be performed is often considerably less than those required when typing. Voice recognition software is available in most of the common languages, including Japanese and Chinese. Perhaps the best-known providers of software have been Lernout & Hauspie, and IBM. We are referring to speech recognition here as a tool of the translator. However, it has much wider implications. If it is sufficiently accurate, it can provide the text version of a speech, which can then be translated into another language by means of sight translation (translation produced orally on the spot). A recent article (Corn, 2000) in the November 2000 issue of *Wired* magazine reports on the use of voice recognition to provide transcripts of congressional hearings.[4]

It also forms a crucial component in Machine Interpretation (MI) systems, such as Verbmobil (see Kay *et al.*, 1994). An MI system consists of the following components:

- Speech recognition software to convert incoming speech to text.
- MT software to translate that text into target language text.
- Speech synthesis software to convert the MT output (text) into the (synthesized) speech of the target language.

Speech recognition software can also be used in the simultaneous translation of text-based chat. It enables the translator to concentrate on the source text as it appears in the chat window, and simultaneously to dictate the translation into the chat window for target language users. Even if a certain amount of editing is required, it will still save time and provide accuracy. As wireless Internet becomes more popular, voice recognition will likely play a major role in user interfaces to wireless Internet devices, and have the potential to support multilingual communication over these devices through simultaneous translation and interpretation.

The teacher of translation and interpretation

Because of the very rapid development of new technologies, the translator and interpreter must become sufficiently adaptable to the new technologies to continue working. For this reason, learning to learn becomes a prime necessity, and the teacher must be as much a facilitator as a provider of knowledge. Both student and teacher must continuously become familiar with new technologies, and teachers can guide students on the basis of their greater experience. Among the universities that are doing an outstanding job in providing the new education are Kent State University in the US, the University of Leeds in the UK, the University of Limerick in Ireland and the University of Maastricht in the Netherlands. More recently, the University of Washington has introduced such a program (Irmler, 2001), and the Monterey Institute of International Studies is also enhancing its translation and inter-pretation technology curriculum. It is instructive to visit the Web sites of these institutions to see how thoroughly they are pursuing technology. In Europe, the EC-sponsored project Language Engineering for Translators Curricula (LETRAC) is indicative of the importance placed on language engineering in the training of translators and interpreters. One of the authors visited the School of Translation at the University of Geneva in 2000 and found that its state-of-the-art lab was equipped with workstations loaded with translation memory systems for regular use by the students.

So, the market reality is increasingly taken into account by educational institutions – at least by some of them. However, both in the USA and Europe, most of these institutions are not geared to deal fully with tools to process non-European languages that require double-byte character sets. In Europe, the 'multilingual information society' tends to mean the society based on European languages. In Asia, the main emphasis tends to be placed between their respective languages and English. For this reason alone, inter-institutional cross-fertilization schemes would be beneficial to accommodate a wider range of languages. Virtual learning with flexible access to different courses in different countries may have a role to play here. We will discuss such training issues in Chapter 8.

In the following section, we consider the implication of the increasing need for language engineering by envisaging a new type of expert.

Translation Engineers

It seems that, as the world becomes progressively wired and instantly connectable, the Internet and its associated communication media are justi-fying the need for language engineering in an unprecedented manner. However, constructing effective and efficient language support in these environments is far from simple. As we have discussed above and in earlier chapters, the engineering approach is becoming essential for the design of a Translation Communication System. In particular, what is becoming clear is the need for language engineers who understand Translation and TMC (Translation-mediated Communication).

In this context, we imagine that a new breed of experts called 'translation engineers' may emerge. They will require two kinds of knowledge and skill: thorough familiarity with the principles and problems of translation, and knowledge of IT in order to support a continuously changing medium of multilingual communication. The role of translation engineers will be to fill the gap between today's translators (who do not understand technical issues beyond using word processing programs and the Internet for background research) and language engineers (who may have computational linguistics or engineering background, but do not have knowledge or skills in Translation in specific languages). This group of professionals will likely appear among today's language engineers, but with specialized training on Translation and TMC. Language engineering will clearly be an inevitable future for Translation, not in the sense that all language support will be automated, but in the sense that engineering solutions will increasingly become an integral part of Translation communication systems.

In the next chapter we will examine CMC in order to observe how Messages are changing as a result of the changes in modalities of communication.

Topics for Further Research or Discussion

(1) Try experimenting with various online MT systems. Start with an English text and translate it into first Spanish and then from Spanish into Portuguese. Then back-translate the Portuguese into English. Finally, work with combinations of languages that are not close to each other, such as English–Japanese–Chinese–English. In what situations do you obtain output that could be edited with relatively little work? In what cases would it be a waste of time?

(2) Try out various translation memory systems through generic demonstration versions that may be available through the vendor's Web site on the Internet. The leading vendors include Trados (http://www.trados.com), Star (http://www.star-group.net) and SDLX (http://www.sdlintl.com).

(3) Think about the benefit of using speech recognition systems from the point of view of both the language support provider and the user.

Notes

1. For an extensive treatment of the technology involved in this and other related developments, visit the news release from Microsoft Corporation, 'Microsoft

Research: Natural Language Processing Hits High Gear,' at http://www. microsoft.com/presspass/features/2000/05-03nlp.asp.

2. TRADOS offers a free extraction program in its demonstration program of TRADOS Workbench, which can be downloaded from http://www.trados.com. It has a plug-in for Microsoft Word that allows one to save a Web document, open it in Word and translate the text by replacing the source with the target language.

3. We will use the term 'speech recognition' here to refer to the ability of a computer to recognize speech input from a single individual, which is the most common use of the technology at present. Some dictation software allows for more than one user, but each user must select his/her own name before launching the program. 'Voice recognition' would include the ability to recognize the voice of individual users and, more broadly, the ability to recognize voice input in a particular language from any number of persons.

4. See 'Filegate.gov' at http://www.wired.com/wired/archive/8.11/govdocs.html, and the company that does this work at http://www.hearingroom.com/#.

Chapter 4

Computer-mediated Communication and Translation

We have argued so far that one of the significant impacts of the Internet on Translation is the changing nature of the Message and the way in which it is transmitted, stored and processed. This chapter focuses on Computer-mediated Communication (CMC) to highlight its characteristics in relation to Translation. In particular, we introduce the concept of 'transterpreting' as a hybrid form of translation and interpretation necessary to assist inter-lingual 'chat,' which is interactive 'written' discourse. We also touch on the emerging voice-based communication on the Internet, and its impact on Translation and TMC.

Characteristics of CMC and Translation

Flanagan (1997) categorizes online texts into three general groups of 'reference text,' 'communicative text' and 'interactive text'. Web documents are used for reference and for information dissemination and gathering purposes, and normally form uni-directional communication where the Receiver accesses the site to view already-existing materials. E-mail messages are sent to individuals, forum groups or newsgroups for communicative purposes because they elicit responses. Chat takes place in real-time, mainly via typed text between two or more individuals, although the voice channel is being incorporated in some chat platforms. These CMC modes can also be classified in terms of asynchronous (e.g. Web and e-mail) and synchronous (e.g. chat) CMC. The way the information is presented in each text type ranges from multimedia with hypertext, audio and graphics for the Web to mostly text with e-mail, although the latter allows a link to a Web site, as well as file attachments that may contain multimedia components. While chat was initially text-only, this mode is increasingly incorporating the voice channel, as well as animated graphics such as avatars. Chat with voice mode in effect creates audiographic conferencing, which is equivalent to audio conference with a computer link that provides an interactive whiteboard. ActiveWorlds (see Figure 4.1) is a commercial site that combines text-based and voice-

Table 4.1 CMC according to online text types

Online text category	Reference text	Communicative text	Interactive text
Online text examples	Web documents	e-mail messages	chat messages
Mode of communication	asynchronous		synchronous
Multimedia components used for presenting information	hypertext	linear text with embedded hyperlink	linear text
	2D and desktop 3D graphics, video	emoticons and other ASCII-based images	
		multimedia as attached file, including voice	2D and desktop 3D computer graphics
	audio		voice

based chat with shared virtual environments. Today e-mail and chat functions are also subsumed within the Web structure. Table 4.1 summarizes the main CMC modes most commonly used today according to online text types on the basis of Flanagan (1997).

The following examines features of Web, e-mail and chat in relation to Translation, expanding on the outline given in Chapter 2.

Web

The Web is constructed on the basis of hypertext, in which related information is tagged. The information is stored in different physical locations (servers), but the link is made seamlessly from the user's computer (client) via HTTP (Hypertext Transfer Protocol) using the point-and-click mechanism. Web texts cover a wide range of topics. Most commercial sites are written grammatically with few spelling or punctuation errors, while personal sites provided by individuals may contain factual as well as grammatical errors.

The Web creates a demand for translation from essentially two sources: the readers and the providers of Web sites. Readers, or what we call Receivers of the Message, require a given Web page to be in their language to allow for real-time browsing and information gathering. Site providers or 'Senders of the Message' target specific audiences by localizing their sites into the Receiver's language and cultural conventions. Certain unique aspects of Web text pose special challenges for language facilitation.

Text on the Web displays a more open structure than conventional paper-based linear text. For example, Negroponte (1995: 70) sees hypertext as 'a collection of elastic messages that can stretch and shrink in accordance with the reader's actions.' A Web text may be read in any order, not just from the beginning to the end. This in turn requires translators to take text coherence into consideration, even when the translation is read randomly. For example, the use of pronouns and abbreviations has to be treated with care if a document has links to other sites in various places. Rice (n.d.) further suggests that translators should avoid the heavy use of colloquialisms which may make it harder for some readers to understand the document, as it is often difficult to anticipate the readership of the given Web site. The translated text also needs to look appropriate on screen in terms of style of writing and presentation. For this reason, it is generally advised that the translator should review the translation in hypertext on screen before delivering the work. This requires translators to become familiar with screen-based aesthetics.

Web localization also raises the issue of cultural appropriateness, not only of text but also in relation to non-textual elements that are part of the 'packaging,' as discussed in Chapter 1. Translated text accompanied by unchanged culture-specific icons and symbols may cause confusion on the part of the Receiver in another culture, as it creates an example of correct content but poor packaging. In some cases, this consideration results in a re-design of the whole site. For example, it may change the 'icon/alphabet ratio' (the proportion of pictures to writing), which is associated with getting the message across (Kingscott, 1996), as some cultures are more prone to using images than texts to convey certain messages. In effect, the need for translators to take into account the package, which touches on wider cultural issues, points to a new dimension of their task: to account for non-verbal communication aspects in a broad sense. This issue regarding packaging is discussed in more detail in Chapter 5.

E-mail

By comparison with (unlocalized) Web texts, which tend to have an indiscriminate audience, e-mail is normally directed at particular recipients: either one or several individuals. E-mail messages may be characterized in terms of their similarity to spoken communication, which is likely to contain sentence fragments, misspellings, misused punctuation and online

Table 4.2 Examples of Japanese-specific emoticons

(ˆ · ˆ)	a smile with a dot for a mouth, since it is impolite for women to show their teeth
\(ˆ _ˆ)/	a 'banzai' [cheers] smile with arms upraised in a Japanese gesture
(ˆ ˆ ;)	a cold sweat – among the most commonly used emoticons in Japan
(_o_)	a person sitting with head down and hands stretched in front in a typical gesture for a deep apology

jargon (Herring, 1996). These factors affect the human translation process and make the application of machine translation (MT) particularly challenging. However, e-mail has flexibility in such functions as forwarding, copying or re-sending, normally by pressing just one button, and this could facilitate a seamless link to a translator if the latter is in the digital loop.

Text-based CMC has also introduced a way to express nonverbal communication cues within a text. The ASCII-based codes known as 'emoticons' are extensively used in e-mail and chat to compensate for a lack of contextual information in the form of facial expressions, gestures or tone of voice. These symbols have an implication for translation, as they provide contextual information relevant to the particular message and also because some emoticons are developed in a culture-specific way (Donath, 1997). For example, Table 4.2 shows distinctively Japanese emoticons that are closely tied to physical nonverbal cues used in Japanese communication.

The uniquely Japanese 'cold sweat' emoticon is used in contexts in which the writer of the message is concerned that the message in question may offend the recipient. This directly reflects the Japanese style of communication, which values the sign of modesty that indicates that the writer of the message fears that the message may be too opinionated (Sugimoto & Levin, 2000). This is still a relatively new area of study, particularly in relation to Translation, and conventions on how to deal with emoticons in translation have not yet been established.

As an asynchronous medium of communication, e-mail by definition does not necessitate synchronous translation. And yet, in reality, the Receiver of a message in an unfamiliar language will probably want to have it translated without delay. Similarly, the Sender may decide to have his/her Message translated prior to sending, and this may become an urgent task. It appears that online environments tend to make the time factor critical even for asynchronous exchanges such as forum postings, as explained by Flanagan (1997: 196): 'Much of information online has diminishing value over time; messages posted today rapidly become old news. Users want translations right away, or not at all.' This is why a real-time language solution based on MT has found a niche market.

Chat

One salient characteristic of interactive CMC such as chat is its similarity to spoken discourses as people produce the text as if they are chatting (hence the name 'chat'). As a result, chat texts typically contain many anomalies such as misspellings and grammatical errors. They are also characterized by the use of online jargon and topic fluidity, particularly when chat is used for open social interactions with participants coming and going as they wish. While MT-based chat translation systems have become available on the market (Products and systems, 1997), there appear to be no human-based chat translation services offered. In envisaging such a service, Ashworth (1997) coined the term 'transterpreting' for the modality of Translation required to facilitate inter-lingual chat, which is discussed later in this chapter. As background to this new mode of Translation, we will elaborate on some special characteristics of chat mode.

Chat messages can be characterized by features such as: (1) addressivity (e.g. including the name or abbreviation of the addressee in one's message), (2) abbreviations, (3) paralinguistic and prosodic cues and (4) actions and gestures (Werry, 1996). The last three aspects are to some extent applicable also to e-mail messages. According to Werry, a marked use of addressivity is observed in chat sessions in order to keep turn-taking smooth and avoid confusion as chat often involves multi-party conversations taking place in parallel, with each group discussing a different topic. When parallel communication threads are running among multiple participants who are identifiable only through the text, it is essential to specify to whom the message is addressed. This becomes a relevant point in a transterpreting practice, and is discussed later.

The second set of characteristics concerns CMC-specific abbreviations. Examples may include IMHO (in my humble opinion) or TTYL (talk to you later). The reason for their use is attributed to 'screen size, average typing speed, minimal response times, competition for attention, channel population and the pace of channel conversations' (Werry, 1996: 53). In other words, abbreviation makes for compactness and brevity and is therefore easier to type, in turn achieving a higher response speed. This suggests that the translator serving this mode of communication requires knowledge of such abbreviations in both the source and target languages. Another feature of synchronous CMC designed to cut typing time is 'key binding' whereby a frequently used phrase or image can be stored and retrieved by pressing a single key. Similar functions can be useful for the translator who in turn can speed up his or her keyboard entry. This is particularly useful in view of the fact that delay in chat message transmission (which may be caused by high Internet traffic or by technical limitations within the host or the client computers) often disrupts the flow of communication. In a typical chat session, a lag greater than five seconds causes the conversation to 'lose any sense of realism' and 'the turn taking falls out of order' (Marvin, 1995). In our experience, this is also applicable to voice-based chat. The provision of language facilitation in this environment clearly needs to be sensitized to the timing issue as the facilitation process itself inevitably introduces further delay.

Another factor relevant to language facilitation in this environment is the use of so-called online jargon, including abbreviations, and its role as a sign of membership. As noted by Marvin (1995), the special symbols and vocabulary mark the insider status because they demonstrate knowledge and skill, which are requirements of belonging to the given group. Specialized vocabulary such as 'lurking', 'teleporting' and 'morph' may be baffling to newcomers whose very lack of jargon easily reveals their inexperience of a given CMC environment. Smooth language facilitation will therefore require a certain familiarity with these conventions on the part of the translator. The third point, about 'paralanguage and prosodic cues' reflects the innovative use of linguistic devices such as capitalization, spelling and punctuation, which create auditory effects in written text. For example, capitalization indicates shouting, whereas a word such as 'aaiiee' with any number of letters a, i and e illustrates shock or dismay (Marvin, 1995). Other words with particular spelling as in 'sokay,' 'bout' and 'gonna' reflect spoken American English.

The evolution of the special language use relates both to pragmatics and to membership identification. Where such groups operate across language boundaries with the aid of translators, it will be important that the translators be familiar with the conventions observed by the group. These conventions may be established over time as an online register as one kind of sublanguage.

The fourth feature concerns the use of words and visual images to symbolize 'gestural qualities of face-to-face communication' (Werry, 1996). For example, in IRC (Internet Relay Chat), commands called 'emote' or 'pose' are also used, allowing one to add actions described in words. A command such as 'emote laughs uncontrollably' results on the screen as '[name of the person] laughs uncontrollably.' Rheingold (1995: 148–49) explains their functions: 'It [emoting] adds a new dimension to your communications... poses give you some added control over the atmosphere in which a conversation takes place – a taste of the all-important context that is often missing from words alone.'

In terms of compensating for nonverbal communication cues, some chat sites use eye-catching animated computer graphics such as Microsoft's ComicChat™ and ActiveWorlds™. These environments demonstrate the increasing sophistication of computer graphics and avatars with a growing range of facial expressions and gestures to express nonverbal cues, as illustrated in Figure 4.1.

ComicChat automatically creates default comic strip scenes with individual characters displaying a number of facial expressions, while ActiveWorlds uses animated avatars, which the user can move around various virtual environments. In some of these graphics-based chat envi-

Screen shot reprinted by permission from ActiveWorlds.

Screen shot reprinted by permission from Microsoft Corporation.

Figure 4.1 Avatars in ActiveWorlds and a scene from ComicChat

Table 4.3 New modes of translation required for inter-lingual CMC

Online text category	Reference text	Communicative text	Interactive text
New modes of language support	Web localization, Web MT	e-mail translation by human and MT	transterpreting, chat MT
New dimensions	culturalization including non-textual elements	speech-like text, online jargon, emoticon	same as e-mail and also logistics of how to enable human-based transterpreting

ronments, users are able to select from a range of nonverbal cues to match their texts. Because the Sender actively chooses an appropriate cue, normally from a limited range of expressions, nonverbal communication in CMC environments tends to be deliberate and unambiguous, often unlike the case with face-to-face interactions. These are new and emerging modes of communication of particular relevance to TMC. Very little translation research has yet been conducted in this area. Table 4.3 summarizes the new modes of language facilitation linked to CMC according to the online text type discussed earlier.

Of the three forms of new modes of language support, Web localization is the most well established service to date, whereas human-based e-mail or chat translation services do not seem to have been developed in any substantial way. However, there are MT-based solutions offered for each of the online text categories. As discussed in Chapter 3, this points to the fundamental affinity of MT with online texts. However, Web localization work involves culturalization (see Chapter 5) and generally seeks a Receiver-focused high-quality translation as provided by human localizers and translators. By comparison, Web MTs cater to the need for language assistance for information-gisting purposes. In this way, new modes of communication drive a new Translation service and also new Translation modalities may be created, as in the case with transterpreting.

Transterpreting as a New Mode of Translation

An early example of extending an interpreting service to the text-based chat environment was demonstrated in the Community Access 96 conference held in November 1996 in Nova Scotia, Canada in which computer conferencing was used to connect remote participants via IRC (Ashworth, 1997). The conference was conducted in Canada's two official languages,

English and French. Registered participants who did not attend the conference in person could view the transcript of the speeches in both languages. In addition, they could discuss the topics among themselves via chat, and submit questions to the attendees. These were interpreted by having an interpreter stand behind a typist, who would type in the translation provided by the interpreter.

About one month prior to this development, Ashworth (1997) conducted a pilot experiment, which he called 'transterpreting' in which, unlike the above example, the translated text was input directly by the 'transterpreter.' It was designed to test the feasibility of having humans mediate text-based chat sessions, particularly those involving languages that use non-ASCII characters such as Japanese and Chinese. The experiment was set up to mediate two separate chat sessions, one between English and Japanese and the other between English and Chinese. The transterpreter used two terminals, each of which showed the chat dialogue in a single language. This was to overcome the character encoding problems (see Chapters 2 and 3) that make it difficult to display single-byte, and double-byte characters side by side (unless one could use a Unicode-based platform, which was not available). Each chat participant therefore saw only the translated chat line from the respective partner. In this study, Ashworth realized the difficult problems involved in trying to provide simultaneous transterpreting, particularly between English and Chinese. Japanese was also a problem, but not as severe as Chinese. This was caused by the time it takes to encode (input) Chinese, which is normally significantly longer than it is for Japanese. Until more efficient input methods are developed and accepted widely, chat itself is cumbersome in Chinese, let alone transterpreting it.[1]

Building on this initial trial, Ashworth designed follow-up experiments, involving both authors. One of the authors acted as a transterpreter for a Japanese chat session in which three English-speaking observers among the group of five participants required translation assistance, mainly from Japanese into English. The chat participants were in different locations: one in Nagoya (Japan), one in Haverford (USA) and three in Honolulu (USA), while the transterpreter was in New Zealand. The chat environment used was a Web-based platform called eWeb, which the transterpreter accessed via dial-up Internet connection using 33.6 kbps modem with the other participants linking either via university T1 connections or via dial-up links. The configuration is illustrated in Figure 4.2, which shows only the Sender of the Message, the transterpreter and the Receiver (although there were three other participants).

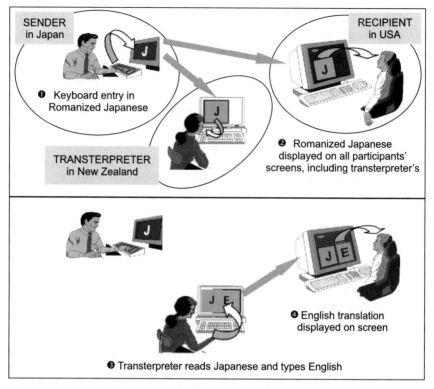

Figure 4.2 Transterpreting experiment

Given that not all participants had access to the Japanese text-processing capability on their computers, Romanized Japanese was used. Both the transterpreter and the translation receiver set up two copies of the eWeb side by side on their respective computer screens so that the chat in progress could be followed by the transterpreter as well as by the translation receivers. This arrangement was necessary to enable them to observe the progress of the chat (even where the Japanese inputs could not be understood by the translation receivers), and also to allow the translation receivers to read the English words that were occasionally used directly by the chat participants.

From the transterpreter's perspective, the above experiments highlighted the following points:

- Real-time transterpreting by a human transterpreter was feasible in practice for chat sessions using today's technology.

- Squeezing two eWeb windows within a 16 inch computer screen obscured the transterpreter's view of the dialogue boxes.
- System delay between pressing the return key to send a section of translated dialog and its clearance from the dialog box hindered the subsequent translation input.
- Reading the Romanized Japanese was inefficient and time-consuming for the transterpreter who is a native speaker of Japanese.
- The five-to-one participant–transterpreter ratio was found to be too overwhelming at times for the transterpreter to cater to.
- Difficulty in anticipating the pace of the dialog was experienced where participants sometimes responded immediately, but at other times only after a long pause.
- Typing the name of the speaker each time was time-consuming.
- Lack of understanding on the part of the transterpreter of the discussion context, which the participants themselves sometimes shared, caused confusion.

A comment made by the receivers of the transterpreting service indicated that, while the translation was useful, it was sometimes disconcerting to see the delay of the translation against the progress of the source language line.

In view of the problems identified by the experiment, the following points can be suggested for consideration in future transterpreting experiments:

- Use a larger computer screen or two separate screens, one for each language in order to evaluate ergonomics.
- Try a Unicode-based platform to allow the concurrent use of English and Chinese/Japanese character sets.
- Experiment with different transterpreter–participant ratios to find an optimum ratio and use of turn-taking protocols by the participants to alleviate multiple parties responding at once.
- Configure macro keys at the transterpreter keyboard to remove the need to type the name of the Sender of the Message.
- Try a voice recognition system as an alternative to typing by the transterpreter, and see if this increases the speed of text input.
- Provide a briefing session or make available a past log in order to increase the transterpreter's familiarity with the context of discussion.
- Introduce a virtual whiteboard function in order to observe how the transterpreter copes with extra information load.

The mode of transterpreting demonstrates convergence of written text-based translation and speech-based interpretation. Emerging communication environments on the Internet, such as desktop-distributed virtual reality, subsume writing and speaking within the mode of synchronous communication. This suggests that they will require language facilitation for both text and speech, as the participants may freely switch from one to the other. In this environment, the transterpreting mode will be needed.

The next section touches on another emerging trend within Internet-based communication, which may have a significant impact on interpretation and TMC.

Speech Communication on the Internet

Although CMC has so far been mainly text-based, the Internet is also being used for voice communication, which is technically called Voice over Internet Protocol (VOIP). The main advantage of this technology from the users' point of view is the considerably reduced price for international calls as compared with standard circuit-switched calls, particularly in the case of PC-to-PC communication. However, the low cost comes with the trade-off of inconsistent voice quality due to the use of packet switching, which was designed primarily to deliver non real-time data. Recently, the world's telephone companies have been incorporating VOIP into parts of their long-distance networks as a cost-saving measure and, in fact, the most common application of VOIP today is for telephone-to-telephone international calls whereby at least a portion of a call's passage goes through IP networks instead of through circuit-switched networks. According to *The Economist* (2001a), the USA generates the most VOIP traffic, followed by China, and in Japan VOIP now accounts for 12% of all international calls.

For the purpose of instruction, we have experimented with a number of VOIP applications based on PC-to-PC platforms and have found that in general they do not deliver the level of quality required for interpretation (see Chapters 7 and 8). However, PC-based voice communication has an advantage in having an extra channel of communication that is not available with the standard telephone: this is the real-time text chat application. It means that if the caller (the Sender) needs to write down something, such as an address or a telephone number, for the benefit of the Receiver, the chat window can be used concurrently while voice communication is in progress. Furthermore, most voice applications allow the text chat channel to be set up only with a specified party in the group. These functions could be useful for language facilitation purposes, in effect creating a channel for the 'whispering' mode of interpreting.

Another major development in terms of speech on the Internet is wireless access from mobile phones. Europe and North America have adopted Wireless Application Protocol (WAP) as the standard technology, while Japan developed its own standard and service known as i-mode. The wireless Internet service or Web phone is expected to be a significant development over the next few years as the world's telecommunication companies move into the third generation (3G) networks that allow broadband Internet access. This enables data transmission over mobile devices of such content as music and moving pictures as well as text.

Web phone subscribers are able to browse Web sites, exchange e-mail messages or engage in interactive games while they are on the move. Search engines such as Google and Excite are moving into this new environment and thereby providing search capabilities equivalent to those available with PC-based Internet access. The main rationale for wireless Internet access is the location-independence it gives for the user. Several translation operators have already announced WAP-based services (e.g. see http://www.ilanguage.com), which can be accessed from Web phones. Given that mobile phones are primarily for speech communication, the implication of this convergence between wireless communication and the Internet is the increased use of voice for CMC on the Internet. So, for example, it will be possible to write an e-mail message by talking to the phone and the message will then be converted to text by speech recognition technology, or an e-mail may be sent containing the voice message itself. With the promised increase in processing capacity of the Internet networks with the Internet II and also wireless networks with 3G (*The Economist* 2001a; Kahney, 2000), we can assume that future CMC will allow full-fledged multimedia. This in turn will mean the need for language support not only for translation but also for interpretation. For example, the i-mode service provider NTT DoCoMo in its Vision 2010 describes a future service including a global mobile conferencing service with simultaneous interpreting (Hadfield, 2000). This kind of scenario will necessitate language support based on teleinterpretation, which we will consider in Chapter 7.

It is relevant at this point to remind ourselves of the ways in which the Web 'justifies itself,' i.e. functions in ways that were not possible earlier, but have certain advantages. This argument relates to Marshall MacLuhan's (1994) notion of the 'rear-view mirror,' according to which new media often grow out of older forms and, in the beginning, serve as mere substitutes – albeit with some advantages. For example, word processors replaced the typewriter for composing letters, but they were printed and signed by the writer and sent via regular mail, even if the recipient had an e-mail address. Admittedly, the volume of this kind of mail has decreased, now being limited to documents requiring notarization and/or personal signatures.

Online text chat, for example, can allow two parties to communicate in text mode, where face-to-face spoken conversation would be stressful – as with arguments between two people and mediations of disputes by a third party in real-time, some kinds of interviews, and the like. Voice chat, accompanied by text chat, allows group members to exchange messages in text mode while listening to the others, and to integrate these messages into the overall discussion. In TMC, language support would use various channels to translate these messages to those participants requiring language assistance. Virtual whiteboards would also fit into this kind of scenario. We will further explore future scenarios of language support in Chapter 9.

This chapter has examined CMC in relation to Translation and TMC. We have suggested that new modes of communication drive the need for new modes of Translation and also provide a new platform on which such language facilitation can be supported. Another relevant dimension, we have come to realize, is the impact of culture on technology adaptation. The Japanese use of e-mail does not seem identical to that of the Americans, while Chinese speakers may not always find text chat liberating and useful mainly owing to technical constraints. Each culture seems to adapt to new ways of communicating on the basis of their particular cultural context. These aspects point to the complexity of globalization, which cannot proceed without due consideration for individual Receiver cultures. Similarly, translation is evolving in the matrix of globalization and its ensuing requirements for localization as culturalization. The next chapter further elaborates on this apparently paradoxical matrix.

Topics for Further Research or Discussion

(1) If we conduct a content analysis of Webs in two languages in a similar category (e.g. catalog sales, virtual malls, corporate Web sites), what patterns of difference of expression do we find, in terms of the use of graphics and icons (packaging) vs. straight text, or the amount of scrolled text vs. linked text? (We are referring here to the habit of making pages smaller by titling and linking paragraphs rather than scrolling down to find them.)

(2) Content analysis of e-mail and chat. Analyze ongoing chats, to see what differences exist between two languages in the use of paralanguage (emoticons, capitalization, etc).

(3) Try transterpreting experiments with some of the recommendations we have made for further research. In your view, what would be the most effective way to support a text chat by transterpreting?

Notes

1. It is interesting to note that a new online program for learning Chinese as a Second Language, developed by the National Foreign Language Resource center at the University of Hawaii, deliberately omits chat as a learning support device for precisely that reason: it takes too long to be able to use it efficiently.

Chapter 5

Globalization and Localization: Culturalization of Content and Package

This chapter examines the impact of globalization on Translation. Globalization has been an on-going process, but its impact on Translation became most obvious when the Internet revealed the extent to which language and culture are a conspicuous barrier to borderless digital communications. In particular, localization is beginning to be seen as an integral part of globalization and accordingly has started to take on a wider meaning than originally intended (see Chapter 1). Localization is now being applied to both the Content and Package of wide-ranging products and services to render the Message as a whole into an appropriate form in the cultural context of the Receiver. We call this process the 'culturalization' of the Message. Furthermore, the emergence of language management as part of a globalization strategy suggests a new approach to Translation with varying levels of language facilitation. This chapter attempts to capture the new dimension of Translation emerging from the impetus provided by globalization and its need for localization.

Globalization and Localization

'Globalization' seems to have many definitions, depending on the particular framework from which it is observed, be it commercial, political, social or technical. In one sense, this reflects the complexity involved in the globalization process and the multitudes of areas it involves. The Localization Industry Standards Association (LISA) defines a 'well-globalized product' to mean a product 'that has been enabled at a technical level for localization' (LISA, 2000). For the purpose of this book, we define globalization in relation to Translation-mediated Communication (TMC) as: 'a process to enable the Message to be adaptable to the condition that may be imposed by Receivers who do not share the same linguistic and cultural backgrounds as the Sender.' In turn, the term 'localization' can be defined as 'a process to facilitate globalization by addressing linguistic and cultural barriers specific to the Receiver who does not share the same linguistic and cultural backgrounds as the Sender.' As such, while localization does not provide all the solutions required for globalization, it clearly holds significant implications.

The recent emergence of the Internet as a context/locus for international communication has resulted in a significant part of business globalization taking place on the Web. This has had a direct impact on localization, in which Web sites must conform to given language and cultural conventions (see Chapter 1). As such, Web localization has come to involve not only the Content of the Message but also that of the Package – such as the general design of the home page, the layout, the font, the color scheme, the icon design and the positions of buttons. In Web localization, the term 'content management' is used to include: (1) localization of the Web site and (2) maintaining the given Web site. It is therefore different from our own use of the term Content. In this chapter, as defined in Chapter 1, we use Content with a capital C to mean specifically 'the words and linguistic structures' of the Message whereas 'Package' includes any other non-textual elements and the container (medium) in which the Content is delivered.

In a sense, certain print media have followed an approach similar to Web localization in terms of modifications made to Content and Package. For example, regional versions of internationally distributed magazines such as *Time* and *Newsweek* are often designed separately with specific local appeal. As a result, they may have different sets of feature articles, covers, layouts and the like. This process can be considered as an adaptation rather than a translation, as is localization, which is a process to adapt the Message to the context of the Receiver environment. Furthermore, adaptation is meant to re-create the Message, to give it the look and feel of the equivalent local product. This has made it necessary for both Content and Package to be transformed. Right from the start, the localization process as applied to computer software was destined to encroach on the dimension of changing the Package. For example, the Japanese localized version of Microsoft Word   has a number of features specific to the Japanese language that are not applicable to, and therefore not found in, its original English-language version. While a certain uniformity is kept across different language and country versions of Microsoft products, each fully-localized product tends to display unique features, as in the case of adaptation rather than translation. We discuss this issue again later in this chapter.

The difference between the regionalized print media and the localized software clearly lies in the digital environment in which the latter is embedded. As discussed in Chapter 2, the digital content lifecycle differs from that of analog/atomic documents. Localization is an anomaly from the perspective of conventional Translation, which primarily concentrated on the conversion of Content and was often constrained in terms of controlling the Package (see Chapter 1). By comparison, in localization, both these aspects become subject to changes. This is partly because the Message subject to localization is typically embedded in the digital environment while in traditional translation the Message normally is in analog form. Whereas digital environments somewhat more readily facilitate modifications of the Package, analog-based communications modes do not have the same ease in the degree of control. While the localizer could adjust 'the look and feel' of a software product in terms of Content and Package to suit the Receiver, conventional Translation has generally been stuck with the largely pre-determined Package that consists of two-dimensional text and fonts for translation and speaking voice, and certain nonverbal cues for interpretation in delivering the Message. Digital multimedia environments could allow extreme changes in Package by modifying text, backgrounds, images or sounds to the desired extent.

The extensive adaptation of the Message normally employed in localization supports the role of Translation as 'domestication' as opposed to 'foreignization.' Venuti (1995) laments the general tendency of 'a reductive domestication' of foreign literary works translated into English largely motivated by commercial interests. In Japanese publishing circles, there was a clear shift some time ago for translations to adopt the domestication approach. This came after a long history in which Japanese readers generally expected translations to be difficult to read and comprehend, and accepted this as a natural outcome of a translation trying to convey foreign ideas and contexts embedded in the Message. However, the recent change is the result of advocating readability with the Receiver-oriented approach. A term called 'super-translation' (*chou honyaku* in Japanese) even appeared which incorporates a greater component of adaptation into translation. For example, some Japanese translations may even exclude certain chapters that are deemed generally not relevant to local Japanese readers. Super-translation meant an adaptation by way of translation in order to make the text digestible to the Receiver, thus endowing the translator with considerable editorial liberty. In such cases, the translation process involves a dramatic adaptation of the Content itself.

With a medium of communication such as the Web, which online and up to date, instant recognition and digestion of the Message are of paramount importance, and foreignization of the Content just does not fit in with the nature of this medium. As a result, more sophisticated localized sites seem to follow a full domestication approach. However, some sites take a mixed approach by retaining a certain amount of foreignness as a form of novelty appeal to the viewers, partly in hopes of establishing international branding.

In the context of globalization, TMC has generally come to mean Receiver-oriented messaging in the form of localization and implies that both Content and Packaging normally undergo transformation. Figure 5.1 illustrates the relationship between globalization, localization and translation.

The diagram shows how localization is part of globalization and Translation is in turn a component of localization. In one sense, Translation is a core to both localization and globalization, but in another sense, without the engineering inputs of localization, globalization on the Internet is not feasible. The diagram also shows how Translation in general can be seen as more concerned with Content than Packaging whereas in localization Packaging is as important as the Content. As we have been discussing, this seems to reflect the nature of the Message in a digital environment.

Another important concept involved in globalization is internationalization, which normally refers to a technical process to prepare a product for an international market. We will examine its meaning in terms of TMC.

Internationalization and TMC

We introduced the basic concept of internationalization in Chapter 2. Here, we will further elaborate on the significance of this process in TMC. The process known as internationalization has been used in the software industry as a way to employ a single design of a given product throughout its international markets. It has meant using English as a lingua franca with

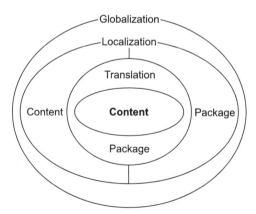

Figure 5.1 Globalization, Localization and Translation with Content and Package conversions

the product design largely based on North American or Anglo-Saxon cultural conventions. However, more recently internationalization has been used to detect and eliminate upstream, hard-to-localize elements for a given product that is subsequently to become localized into regional versions. Technically, this involves separating text and source code for ease of handling by the localizer when the text is submitted for translation. The product also needs to be designed to support particular character sets, as discussed below. The internationalization approach has also become important with the increasing requirements to have Web sites localized into a wide range of languages and then to have such sites managed. The most significant point about internationalization from the perspective of translation is that it places concern for translation right at the outset of globalization planning – a clear contrast with the traditional attitude towards translation as an afterthought and an isolated activity. We will concentrate on the non-technical aspects of the internationalization process, which concerns linguistic and cultural aspects.

Translation has traditionally been carried out within the constraints of the conditions given by the client (the Sender, the Receiver or a separate commissioner) of the particular work and the factors inherent in the Message itself. The internationalization process attempts to consider the latter aspects at the onset of Message creation, implying that at least some of the constraints are to be eliminated. This affects the concept of TMC considerably. Figure 5.2 illustrates TMC, focusing on the change in the Message [M1] transformed to [M'] by the internationalization process before it is translated by the Translator into [M2].

The Message as [M'] is still in the source language, but is considerably more amenable to the ensuing translation/localization process (see also Figure 2.3). The internationalization process to convert [M1] into [M'] now creates a new type of pre-translation work. In fact, this may remind some

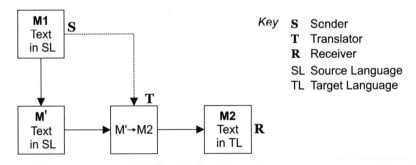

Figure. 5.2 TMC with internationalization

readers of the 'pre-editing' process routinely applied to texts to be processed by Machine Translation (MT) to make them more 'machine-friendly' by eliminating known difficulties such as ambiguities and complexities. However, pre-editing for MT is carried out primarily to simplify the machine translation process, while internationalization (as far as its non-technical aspects are concerned) aims at human consumption and involves changing not only the Content but also the Package. For example, internationalization applied to a Web site will consider the overall design features aside from the text itself. This may also involve considerations from the usability perspective, as discussed by Nielsen (1999). For example, the unit of time (e.g. GMT, UPT), a convention of expressing dates (e.g. 4/5/2000 or 5/4/2000 for April the 5th in 2000), punctuation in expressing decimal points (e.g. $4,000 or £4.000). So, who is doing internationalization? In reality, such tasks are often undertaken by localization engineers, specialized consultants and now increasingly by the new 'globalization solution companies.' Given that cultural aspects strongly enter the picture, in addition to the technical adjustments, the expertise required for internationalization suggests a new skill set. This touches on the issue of a new profession, which we will discuss in Chapter 9.

Culturalization of Content and Package

When text for translation moved from a paper-based to a digital medium such as computer software, the process came to be called localization, as it required special engineering adjustments in addition to translation of texts. Furthermore the nature of the text has changed from static print-based documentation to include online text (such as online menus and Web documents). Localization is now further extending its scope in the context of globalization, particularly on the Internet platform. In order to highlight new dimensions introduced to Translation by localization, we treat localization as culturalization of the Message, as the word 'culture' tends to embrace wider aspects than simply the linguistic issue of converting text into the target language. Since in Chapter 1 we have already outlined what is involved in Web localization, here we will concentrate on what we consider as culturalization aspects involved specifically in Web localization.

Character encoding

The first stage involved in culturalization is text processing in a given language, and this remains a persistent problem that will continue to hamper the localization process as increasing numbers of languages appear on the Internet. Not all languages that are printed in analog environments are digital-ready in terms of their character sets and encoding systems to allow electronic manipulations. In particular, those languages that use character sets outside ASCII have tended to be considered anomalous. As late as 1996, many companies 'going global' did not have a clue as to the difficulties facing them if they wanted to localize their Web sites into languages that use the double-byte character sets. As discussed in Chapters 2 and 3, even today, in 2001, digital publishing in all languages of the world is by no means a reality yet (see Hopkins, 2001; Lommel, 2001). The movement to establish Unicode requires an acceptance at the grass roots level of electronic publishing worldwide. However, it seems as if the toughest problem to overcome is of a political and cultural nature. For example, its approach known as 'unification' of certain Han characters among CJK has caused heated debate (see Sakamura, 1995), as it meant some compromise for accepting slight differences in the shape of characters. This is another kind of culturalization and demonstrates how cultural issues run deep and can hamper globalization.

This issue directly concerns translators now that they have to be involved in text processing, including receiving, displaying, saving and delivering text in a digital environment. Furthermore, the use of software such as speech recognition and speech synthesis, which make speech and text interchangeable, complicates the issue further as it requires a streamlined text-processing environment.

Design and usability

Usability issues touch on the overall design of the Web site, ranging from how to access a certain language version to the position of various function buttons. It also concerns to what extent localization is necessary. In some cases, localization may be carried out only partially, with certain information translated, and in other cases full localization may be considered as the only appropriate measure. Such decisions may be made on the basis of an organization's overall globalization strategy. The design features may include such aspects as the position of function buttons that may need to be modified, for example, when used in bi-directional languages such as Arabic, which reads from right to left, places various buttons on the right-hand side rather than the left and places scroll bars on the left. Ethnographic comparisons of Web sites reveal certain unique characteristics in terms of non-textual elements. The design and usability issue may also involve such aspects as culturally preferred payment methods, for example, in Business to Consumer (B2C) sites. For example, Japanese B2C sites typically offer, in addition to standard credit card payments, cash on delivery or a customer pick-up system at the nearest nationally-known convenience store (O'Hagan, 2000a). These adjustments become important and relevant to the localization exercise.

Branding

Culturalization of the Content draws on the knowledge of target language and cultural conventions relevant to the field to which the text belongs. This process also touches on wider commercial considerations, such as the treatment of brand names in a particular market. While this issue has been applicable to the products and services in offline environments, in the online world (with its generally rapid cycle of information development and launch) this aspect could easily be overlooked. The search engine provider Ask Jeeves™, whose name is immediately recognizable as a trusty butler in most of the English-speaking world, could not assume recognition in other countries. Market research conducted in preparation for the launch of a fully localized Japanese site showed that the butler Jeeves is largely unknown to Japanese consumers although they are familiar with the concept of a butler (Keynote, 2001). In this case, the company eventually decided to leave the name as it is in the hope of following successful prior cases such as Kentucky Fried Chicken's 'Colonel.' Other examples where the particular name sounds actively offensive or means something completely different in the target language would require re-consideration of naming. This type of work therefore requires expertise in the commercial field, such as international market research and multicultural advertising that can provide advice on wider issues than immediate translation problems.

Graphical presentations

One of the aspects that have been highlighted by the localization of Web sites involves the various graphical representations that are present in addition to text. Icons that are based on the nonverbal communication cues of a particular culture may require modifications in order to be appropriate and relevant to the Receiver from a different culture. For example, the show of a palm, certain hand gestures, or specific metaphors based on popular sports in the Sender's country need scrutinizing in the cultural context of the Receiver.

As was illustrated in Figure 5.1, the nature of the work changes between translation and localization, with the former focusing for the most part on the Content, whereas the latter at least places a similar weight on both Content and Package manipulation. As the Internet population shifts outside of the USA and into non-English-speaking countries, the norm of Web design will become hard to pin down. Multinationals currently seem to follow either a decentralized or a centralized model. The former tends to produce regionally unique Web sites with the minimum uniformity between different regions (e.g. see http://www.citibank.com), while the latter conforms to a certain uniform style with varying degrees of region-based styles (e.g. see http://www.microsoft.com; http://www.ibm.com). With its digital flexibility and global reach, the Web is being used as an interactive shop front for a business, rather than as static business brochures. This in turn is widening the scope of the localization process from the limited flexibility pertinent to atomic print media to encompass Content and Package, as well as asynchronous and synchronous communication modes. In other words, the Message subject to localization is likely to undergo multidimensional changes.

Language Management and Levels of Language Facilitation

While language service providers are being transformed to cater to the new demand, the user side is also changing. This is in part to keep complex globalization and localization processes and costs under control. Providing an e-commerce structure in a number of multilingual sites requires good management. Although initially it was believed that the Internet or the Web as a platform for globalization provides a relatively low-cost entry to the given market, some of the world's largest companies are finding that this is simply not true. This has led to the implementation in some organizations of language management as part of globalization strategies.

One example of this can be seen with the approach taken by Microsoft, which uses language facilitation at differing levels, depending on the importance of the particular market. As one of the biggest localization service users, Microsoft draws a substantial proportion of its income from the sales of localized products (Brooks, 2000). Its strategies with localization provide a new direction for language management in the context of globalization. The key feature is the matching of the extent of language facilitation with market profiles in terms of its commercial significance. For example, Microsoft applies three incremental levels of facilitation consisting of what they call Enabling, Localization and Adaptation as described below:

First level: *Enabled* – users can compose documents in their own language, but the software user-interface and documentation remain in English.

Second level: *Localized* – the user-interface and documentation are translated, but language-specific tools and content remain in English.

Third level: *Adapted* – the linguistic tools, content, and functions of the software are revised or re-created for the target market. (Brooks, 2000: 49)

At Microsoft the largest markets, such as Japanese, German and French, will have products adapted for them while small but growing markets, such as Portuguese, Arabic and Hungarian, will see products localized. For emerging markets, such as Thai, Romanian and Vietnamese, only core products are localized (Brooks, 2000). The sophistication and extent of detailed language facilitation diminishes in descending order from adaptation, to localization and finally enabling. This is a novel approach to Translation that has been typically fixed in converting the source text into the target text on one level except for cases where only summary or selective translations or drafts were requested. The example of Microsoft's approach demonstrates the most sophisticated form of Translation as adaptation – which we have called culturalization of Content and Package. Figure 5.3 depicts language management as employed by Microsoft based on the depth of language facilitation directly linked to the market significance:

With this strategy, TMC takes place at varying levels. In fact, the first level of facilitation as enabling does not involve Translation in its traditional sense, as the given software product is mainly adjusted at a technical level to allow inputs in the script of a given language. At the second level of language facilitation, the Message is converted into the Receiver's linguistic environment and a degree of cultural adjustment may be made in terms of basic features. The third level means that the Message is fully adapted to the Receiver's linguistic and cultural environments. A similar strategy can be seen in Web localization, where some organizations opt for

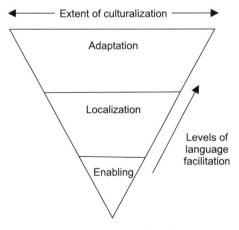

Figure 5.3 Language management with levels of language facilitation (Microsoft model)

partial localization rather than full localization. Such approaches to language management point to the changing notion of the role of Translation in relation to the treatment of the Message in TMC. In other words, the previously dominant single-level conversion model of Translation from the source language into the target language is no longer sufficient. With language management increasingly adopted by the client of Translation, the Message is subjected to Translation strictly under the terms of the client (normally the Sender of the Message in the case of localization), and the client determines the level of facilitation to be undertaken by the Translator. It seems that the force of globalization is resulting in sophisticated localization practice carefully adjusted by the organization's globalization strategies. In this way, products are manipulated in the way they are introduced to foreign markets. For example, user experience of Microsoft products will differ according to different markets as the products are presented with varying degrees of language facilitation.

In the case of major communication media such as telephone or the Internet, the way they finally become accepted by the receiving country seems to be deeply influenced by cultural contexts. As a case in point, the following section looks into the unique manner in which the Internet rather belatedly made inroads into Japan.

Culturalization of Technology: The Case of i-mode

While the Internet has steadily become the mainstream communication medium in most developed countries since the mid-1990s, Japan is considered to have been slow in its adoption of the Internet. However, the introduction of a wireless Internet service 'i-mode' (see Chapter 4) seems to have finally, and rather unexpectedly, launched the country into the Internet era. In contrast to the slow rate of WAP adoption in major European and North American countries, the number of i-mode subscribers in Japan exceeded 20 million as of March 2001 in the rather short period from its launch in February 1999.

Per-household penetration of PCs connected to the Internet remains relatively low in Japan, partly because of high telephone charges (non-discount, standard charge around JPY20 or 20 cents USD per minute), partly because computers are still not user-friendly and, in particular, because typing on the keyboard does not come naturally for most Japanese. Unlike countries where electric typewriters were household fixtures, the complex Japanese writing system involving tens of thousands of characters delayed the development of easy-to-use portable typewriters in Japan. Although Japanese word processors are now widely used in offices and in some homes, most Japanese are still not proficient in typing. This is one of the socio-cultural conditions that made it less easy for computers to penetrate the market. By comparison, a telephone is much more user-friendly, and typing on a keypad is perceived by many Japanese as less challenging than typing on a keyboard. According to its developer, i-mode terminals are deliberately designed to retain the appearance of a phone, with the built-in Internet access almost hidden as part of the telephone functionality (Matsunaga, 2000). To access the Internet, the user needs only to press the 'i-mode' button. Apparently some users are quite unaware that they are on the Internet. Ironically, by making the Internet technology invisible, it has begun to spread widely.

The tiny screen size of the mobile may have been considered inappropriate for viewing Web sites. However, in certain countries, text messaging over the mobile phone has been extremely popular, particularly among the young and mobile population. In Japan particularly, prior to the mobile phone era, pagers enjoyed great success as a medium for sending text. In fact, the limitation of screen space led to the ingenious use of numbers as phonetically coded messages. An array of pre-installed icons also became vital to effective and succinct messaging. For example, i-mode phones have nearly 200 symbols built in for messaging. The results of a comparative study (Sugimoto & Levin, 2000) suggest a link between the frequent use of icons and emoticons and the Japanese style of communication, as well as the importance to them of nonverbal cues. For example, e-mail sent by the Japanese compared with e-mail sent by Americans contained considerably higher numbers of emoticons (Sugimoto & Levin, 2000).

Another success factor of i-mode is attributed to the fact that the service caters to the idiosyncrasies of Japanese social conditions (Matsunaga, 2000). For example, long hours spent commuting on public transport provide an ideal opportunity for e-mailing, online transactions or Net-based entertainment. And wireless Internet facilitates the Japanese penchant for group activities (Hadfield, 2000). An equally important consideration was the matching of the content and the medium; the mobile phone was recognized as different from the computer in terms of when and how people use it to access information. Furthermore, when one is on the move, one tends to seek a different kind of information than when one is sitting at home or in the office with a PC. For example, information related to the particular locality of the mobile user at a given time was considered to be relevant. In this context, the creators of i-mode targeted the functionality of a knowledgeable hotel concierge assisting out-of-town guests (Matsunaga, 2000).

The greatest advantage of i-mode in terms of usability is the fact that Internet access is 'always-there' whenever the phone is switched on. This compares favorably with the process required to connect to the Internet from a PC. The trade-off is its speed at 9.6 kbps, but i-mode is launching the 3G mobile technology in the near future, which will make high-speed broadband connections available. Economic factors are also part of the successful introduction of technology where users pay per byte of data sent or received, plus a modest monthly charge. Given the high telephone charges in Japan, it often costs much less to convey a message by sending it as e-mail from a mobile using i-mode than by talking over the phone. A 250-character e-mail message costs less than JPY5 (US 5 cents).

Despite the speed of the Internet, adapting a foreign technology does not happen instantaneously. While technology use may have universal aspects across cultures, it is also deeply embedded in the cultural context of each country that is introduced to the new technology. I-mode is expected to globalize its service in the near future, and this will provide an opportunity for us to observe how it will facilitate the process of cultural adaptations by the target markets.

This case study points to one significant aspect relevant to Translation in the context of the ongoing globalization process and its needs for localization as culturalization. True adoption of technology by Receiver countries seems dependent upon how it can be localized into a culturally acceptable form in the Receiver's terms. TMC is becoming embedded in the context of globalization in a wide sense and this is changing the dynamics of language facilitation. The next chapter observes the response of translation operators to these changes, and the way in which teletranslation is developing.

Topics for Further Research or Discussion

(1) As a prospective enterprise planning to move from local to global markets, what modifications do you envisage to enable your Web site to reach other markets effectively? (Hint: search the Web for an obviously locally oriented Web site and consider how you might advise its owners if they wished to go global.)

(2) In moving from a local market to markets in other countries, for each country, what kinds of changes would be necessary to localize your site for those markets? (You might want to use Babelfish/AltaVista to search other countries for sites addressing the same content as in the first question and note any differences/similarities you find between your 'source' site, i.e. the one you are basing the exercise on, and the related sites in the other countries).

(3) If you do not know how to answer these questions, how would you find help in doing so?

Chapter 6

Teletranslation

Since 1996 when *The Coming Industry of Teletranslation* (O'Hagan, 1996) was published, the Internet has reached a critical mass and become a significant communications medium, providing the global infrastructure for electronic commerce (e-commerce). Accordingly, the shape of the teletranslation industry is becoming clearer. Its original definition was a language service for both translation and interpretation provided via telecommunications. In view of the developments to date and future prospects, in this book we re-define 'teletranslation' to mean: (1) translation operated via the Internet and (2) translation of Internet-related content. We treat interpreting separately as teleinterpretation in the next chapter. The present chapter examines teletranslation, particularly in relation to today's typical translation practices, to capture the essence of how translation in the traditional sense is undergoing a transformation.

Teletranslation Redefined

We have discussed recent significant developments taking place in Translation in the advent of the Internet. The Internet has affected the lives of translators in the way they send and receive their work, the tools they use, and the type of work they receive. However, our focus has so far been on leading-edge developments and there may be a gap between this and the way many translators actually work today. For our reality-check, let us meet Doug who works for a medium-sized translation company as a technical translator.

Doug is a senior translator with well over 20 years' experience translating business and technical documents from a number of European languages into English. Doug's work consists of technical documents both for print-based and for digital circulation, such as for Web sites and sometimes PowerPoint presentations. Over the years he progressed from the Wang word processor to different generations of IBM compatibles. He uses Microsoft Word for most of his work now and knows all the basic functions. He is only vaguely familiar with different document tags such as HTML, RTF or PDF. He writes for the company's own Web site, but somebody else converts the document to html format. Similarly, somebody else is responsible for extracting these tags before Doug gets started and usually cleans up the source text he works with. So, he does not have to know technical details. The project manager wants Doug to be able to concentrate on the actual translation work.

Doug occasionally uses the Internet for terminology or background searching, but not to a great extent compared with some of his colleagues. This is partly because Doug has much less need to look up terminology than his less-experienced colleagues do, and partly because his well-worn paper dictionaries (sometimes supplemented by CD versions) are generally adequate. Also occasionally the clients supply terminology lists. The company also has a translator/terminologist who can do terminology searches if he really needs extensive research. He knows how to surf the Net and uses e-mail a lot, but shuns trying out new things, partly because he is too busy and partly because he is not that interested in playing with technology. The company had been introduced to Translation Memory (TM) systems over a year ago, but Doug personally has not found them useful – in fact, they tend to slow him down considerably. Nevertheless, he thinks that sooner or later he will have to learn to use the system. He brushes up his translation skills primarily by doing it and by reading foreign newspapers and magazines (mostly print-based) in languages he deals with and also by attending translators' conferences (in person).

This scenario will be familiar to many translators. Doug represents the figure of an intelligent and sound technical translator, but someone who is not yet fully exposed to the sort of changes we have been describing in this book. Also the company he works for represents an average translation provider that is in transition. It has a Web site, but this is only in English and is not used as a full-fledged online transaction platform other than for receiving occasional initial enquiries. TM is tried out, but the company shows no sign of an integrated management system dealing with extractions, terminology or workflow across the board. Within the company itself there is a digital divide between those translators who are savvy with technology and those who are not. And this may be reflected in the slightly different way they work.

In fact, from the point of view of a translator who has been accustomed to the traditional mode of working, 'virtual' translation companies operating on the Internet may appear to be something of a different breed. The latter's Web sites may offer all the functionality of the traditional translation office and often with additional features: instant quotations upon online request, options to use Machine Translation (MT) in addition to Human Translation (HT), FAQs (frequently asked questions) about services, links to related sites that address language issues, and often a recruitment page for freelance translators and in-house staff. These organizations also tend to offer services, such as Web localization, that are closely linked to the Internet although traditional lines of business may also be pursued. How did these companies develop and how are they related to the more traditional translation services? What are the similarities and differences between the new and traditional translation operators? To help answer these questions and further define what teletranslation is, the following section overviews how the translation industry has changed over time mainly owing to the impact of information technology (IT).

Brief history of emergence of teletranslation

From the mid-1990s, the impact of the Internet has begun to penetrate across many sectors of the economy. For example, the Internet now provides the functionality of the library, music store, bookshop or auction house in virtual space, as contrasted with the physical space that these have traditionally occupied, and people no longer need to rely as heavily on physical transportation as they have done in the past. Virtual classes (Tiffin & Rajasingham, 1995) are beginning to supplement physical classrooms, and the Internet is supporting advances in telemedicine and health care.

In this way, the initially non-commercial Internet has now grown to provide the basis for e-commerce. This has motivated some translation operators to move on to the Internet to make their services globally accessible. While major translation and localization organizations have created a significant cyberspace presence via sophisticated multilingual Web sites in addition to their physical presence in the major cities of the world (these are called 'clicks and mortar' in comparison with 'bricks and mortar' companies), a new breed of translation company has appeared. In every appearance these look like e-commerce companies that are largely funded by venture capitalists. These organizations have invested particularly heavily in creating a virtual presence and a virtual production mechanism to meet global demands. Like most e-commerce companies, innovation for them comes from the extensive use of new technology. They typically operate in a time-zone-independent mode of 24x7 processing (24 hours and 7 days a week), providing services that are concentrated on new areas such as Web localization, Web content creation and management, cultural marketing and consultation. Some of them are now providing globalization solutions. These services have a pool of translators, sometimes including partner companies working from different parts of the world, all linked via the Internet or an enterprise-wide Intranet.

For them most of the operational aspects integrate the virtual world: as a space for supporting the transmission of information and as a location of translations of Web documents and multimedia. Documents follow an all-digital path from their inception to their final distribution, as we discussed with the digital content lifecycle (see Figure 2.2). This contrasts with the conventional piecemeal way in which translation operations had to operate using word processors, fax and the postal system. The teletranslation industry is beginning to evolve as the traditional translation industry re-shapes itself into the Internet age. This means that organizations that constitute today's emerging teletranslation find themselves in varying stages moving towards full-fledged teletranslation. These can be categorized into three main groups according to their maturity towards teletranslation (see Figure 6.1).

The lowest group in the sense of maturity towards teletranslation is what we call POTS. This acronym is normally used in the field of telecommunications to mean Plain Old Telephone Service, but here we mean 'Plain Old Translation Service'. This refers to traditional translation providers that are on the way to teletranslation, as in Doug's company described at the beginning of this chapter. This group is by far the most common in terms of numbers. They may have Web sites as a means of marketing their services, but may not be geared to serve in a truly global manner. For example, their sites may be available only in a single language and may lack true international outlook in terms of workflow, text-delivery mechanisms or charging methods. For these groups, the Web site is often not used as an active channel for full transactions including billing and payment settlements as well as receiving and sending work but rather as a token of their initial participation in online commerce.

The next group, which is closer towards teletranslation, includes multinational localization firms and e-commerce-modeled translation companies with a strong focus on localization. Examples of this group may include Lionbridge (http://www.lionbridge.com) and e-Translate (http://www.etranslate.com) which have physical offices in main centers of the world as well as a strong virtual presence. This group is sophisticated in the use of IT in all facets of its production of translation, and tends to cater to a large number of language combinations (MLVs, as we referred to in Chapter 1) using its strength with global staff and contractors. Such skills as project management are considered of paramount importance, and the translation resources will come both from in-house staff and from outsourced contractors. E-commerce companies that are targeting a specific overseas market and requiring localization expertise are likely to seek these companies as their language support partners.

Much smaller in scale, but nevertheless important, are technology-savvy individual translators who set up their own reasonably sophisticated Web sites through which they operate their businesses. They will routinely use tools such as Translation Memory and be familiar with document tags and computing and telecommunications to the extent that they will be able to deal with documents in different formats, including multimedia. Translators in this group may be highly specialized in one or two areas. An example of one such company is Origin (http://www.origin.to). These translators may be registered with a number of larger companies as well as translation job portals such as Aquarius (http://www.aquarius.net) and Proz (http://www.proz.com). They are also likely to be frequent visitors to virtual communities for translators, such as language-specific translators' mailing lists hosted by eGroups (http://www.egroups.com) or various sites hosted by language industry players (e.g. TranslationZone at http://www.translationzone.com) whereby they can learn the latest technology trends, tools, industry news and the like.

As is already the case, some translators in the above group are developing into comprehensive globalization companies whose services encompass from internationalization to extensive culturalization. These services will be perceived as the highest value-added and will be able to take advantage of the language facilitation needs arising from the continuously evolving Internet and CMC.

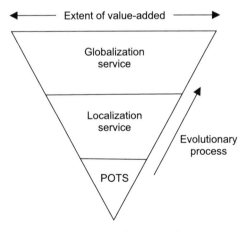

Figure 6.1 Emergence of the teletranslation industry

Figure 6.1 represents the emerging picture of the teletranslation industry in which the electronic network is used to facilitate the customer interface, distribution of text and sometimes the translation function itself, as in the case of online translation services. Furthermore, the main translation work undertaken is also characterized by its direct link to the digital media. Teletranslation can be seen as evolving in response to the need for a language-processing capability to deal with the new types of Messages being developed that are specific to the Internet environment and, at the same time, leveraging the advantage afforded by the worldwide information infrastructure based on the Internet.

The defining characteristics of teletranslation are derived from the digital environment in which it operates and which it serves. In the following sections, teletranslation is examined from the perspective of both the user and the provider. The former is examined on the basis of where in the digital content lifecycle (see Chapter 2) the need for language support occurs. From the provider's side, we will expand and consolidate the outline of the emerging model of teletranslation that we provided in Chapter 1.

Teletranslation from the User's Perspective

From the user's side, the need for language support can be roughly divided into (1) the Sender of the Message as the client where language support is sought mainly for information dissemination purposes, and (2) the Receiver of the Message as the client where the Receiver seeks language support.

(1) The Sender as the client

As was identified earlier, when the Sender of the Message is the client, the purpose of translation is normally for information dissemination. In this case, teletranslation may be employed during the Authoring, Publishing/Distributing or Revising/Updating stages in the digital content lifecycle (see Figure 2.2). This is the most common pattern with localization projects where the Sender of the Message adapts the Message to the Receiver's language and cultural conventions before it reaches the Receiver. The following expands on each case in more detail:

Authoring
When language support is used during this stage, the text is effectively re-created with specific consideration for the Receiver and the presumed subsequent translation difficulties. The Sender wishes to get the message across to Receivers in other language(s) and writes the source document

with this in mind. The Sender also may be sensitive to the possibility that the language in the original text could entail difficulties in the translation process, and composes the text with this in mind. Language support may be combined with the following strategies:

- *In-house style-sheet:* Some organizations have in place a systematic documentation management system that includes the use of a style-sheet for authors to follow for all documentation. This ensures consistency of the use of terminology, and adherence to pre-determined phraseology to some extent to give uniformity of style.
- *Internationalization:* As discussed in detail in Chapter 5, some digital content that undergoes the internationalization process, will effectively apply language support during this stage. The task is of an engineering nature as well as cultural. Some teletranslation organizations are offering globalization solutions, which incorporate internationalization.
- *Controlled language:* Some organizations use controlled language as part of a documentation management system. Controlled language may be considered as the next stage beyond the in-house style-sheet. The application of controlled language used to be common for the purpose of producing 'plain English' for documents to be used in non-English speaking markets. It is now more specifically related to the use of a language-processing system such as MT. Controlled language in effect functions as 'pre-editing' of text to render the Message more amenable for subsequent translation by computer.

Publishing/distributing

Language support is most typically commissioned in the stage after authoring and before publishing/distributing. In these cases, the source content normally has not been internationalized and the language support tends to be sought independently from the Message creation. This is typical of conventional translation where the Message contains elements that are inherently difficult to render in a form suitable to the Receivers' environments. On a technical level, dealing with online text may make it necessary to remove or separate out various document tags before the translation task can take place. At least in some cases, the translator needs to have some understanding of these tags, although there are now increasing numbers of tools available to take care of tags (see Chapter 3).

Revising/updating

One of the unique and common features of digital content is the requirement for regular changes, as in the case of news and newsletter updates.

Web sites whose information relies on its newness will go through these updates, and accordingly language support needs to incorporate all such changes. This becomes complex in terms of management and workflow, particularly when multiple languages are involved.

(2) The Receiver as the client

In comparison with the above pattern, when the Message is not in the Receiver's language, the Receiver often seeks language support for information-gathering purposes. Language support may be employed for the Accessing, Comprehending or Activating stages in the digital content lifecycle. These circumstances often require real-time language support online. This is why MT-based services are typically used, particularly for a first-pass translation.

Accessing

Search engines have become an indispensable tool for accessing information online, and this is the situation when language support is often sought. Many search engines have responded to this requirement by incorporating MT systems, so that the search results can be translated directly without the user leaving the online environment, or the search engines themselves have been localized to allow inputs in different languages. Some details of these solutions have been examined in Chapter 3.

Comprehending

The Receiver may conduct information search online and wait until later to look at the gathered information. This will create the situation where the Receiver re-visits the given site or information offline and discovers it to be in an unfamiliar language, triggering the need for language support. The Receiver may then use some sort of MT system either on the desktop or online, or a human-based service.

Activating

The Receiver may accept a cursory understanding of the Message initially, but when specific actions need to be taken based on the gathered information, language support may be sought. For example, the Receiver may decide to order a book online and this action may necessitate language support, say, to fill out a form. At this point the Receiver may decide to use language support.

As can be seen, teletranslation may be applied at any of the above nodes in the digital content lifecycle. This illustrates the far-reaching impact of introducing a global e-commerce site that requires language support consideration in all the above nodes. Keeping such user needs in mind, the following section examines the provider's perspective according to the critical factor categories provided in Chapter 1.

Teletranslation from the Provider's Perspective

(1) Speed

When the Receiver of the Message is the client, the need for language support tends to occur online or in near real-time. This requirement has highlighted the affinity between MT and the Internet (see Chapter 3). MT is fast, cheap and compatible with the digital environment. The speed factor also affects localization where the Sender is the client and the requirement for language support is not real-time, but the time allowed for translation seems to be becoming shorter. Also when the software publisher is attempting simship (simultaneous shipment), the delay in completion of one language version significantly affects the other localized products. The only option left for human-based language support is to facilitate the human process by using technology in all areas of production.

(2) IT-device friendliness

The development of wireless Internet access is creating the need for language support to be accessible from mobile devices. WAP-based (see Chapter 4) language services already exist, but are at an early stage of development. Whatever medium the Internet access moves in, language support needs to fit into the new environment. Teletranslation is currently mainly based on the Web platform on PC, but needs to be adaptable to new environments such as WAP and i-mode as they become a popular mode of global communication. This is particularly applicable to certain countries, which are typically deprived of Internet access (i.e. on the other side of the digital divide), and are perhaps more likely to first have access to wireless technology. Development of translation procedures for these languages will then become necessary. Furthermore, the lack of character-encoding systems for minority languages may in some cases drive the use of voice instead of text (e.g. sending voice-mail instead of text). These requirements demand technical expertise to design and build teletranslation interfaces in an appropriate mode.

(3) Quality

Quality has always been an issue with language support and it has often been regarded as not readily measurable. This notion is changing particularly in the advent of the localization industry with which quality control of products meant measuring the quality of translation (localization). The need for quantifying the quality comes from the increasing project size and complexity of the nature of processing involved in a job. As a result, organizations such as LISA have produced their own Quality Assurance models (see http://www.lisa.org), which include QA tools. This allows organizations to introduce objective (repeatable and reproducible) measures to assess quality (see Fry, 1999). A similar approach is needed for Web localization, given that it reaches a much larger group of Receivers than does translation based on print media with its physical distribution. Furthermore, the quality of translation of digital media tends to include not just the textual component, but also non-textual elements. As discussed in Chapter 5, the quality of teletranslation will increasingly be judged in terms of both Content and Package, with the latter becoming a much more explicit factor. Subjective and entirely manual quality control and quality assurance methodologies are becoming inadequate in this context.

(4) Pricing

The digital Message requires language facilitation for both Content and Package. This makes it difficult to charge on a per-word basis, which worked well with traditional translations and print-based media. Furthermore, tools such as Translation Memory (TM) make the source language word-count-based charging inapplicable if the translation service provider needs to discount strictly for the portion of translation supplied by TM. In the area of software localization, there is a suggestion (LISA, 2000) for a new charging method in terms of royalties, based on sales of the localized product. Another factor that needs to be considered is proliferation of free translation services such as those typically provided using MT.

(5) Mixed modality of text and voice

The Internet has introduced new modes of communication such as e-mail and chat. From the point of view of language support, such Messages require a mixed modality of translation and interpretation. In particular, in order to facilitate an inter-lingual chat session, it is necessary to translate in real-time a speech-like dialogue, albeit in text form. The need for language support for mixed modality may also arise from technology (such as speech recognition and synthesis systems) that makes speech and text interchangeable. For example, some programs, such as Paltalk™, which is widely popular in the Middle East, have chat rooms with both voice chat and simultaneous text chat. When these are employed for a serious purpose such as an online meeting, the teletranslators must attend to both modalities in some fashion. Additionally, the availability of voice recognition/dictation systems can make it possible for the teletranslator to post text translations of text chat very rapidly by dictating and copy/pasting the text into the chat space.

(6) Value-addedness

The value added by translation has traditionally not been clear cut, as evidenced from its charging system; word-based pricing does not relate the value of translation to the accrued value of the resultant translated Message. The value-addedness resulting from localized software products is fairly clear, as is that of localized Web sites – whose value should be obvious from the number of hits to that site. The localization industry is addressing this issue, and this is reflected in the review of the pricing methods discussed above. Furthermore, with the Message for translation becoming clearly inclusive of both Content and Package, the value-addedness is now obtained by integrating engineering work into translation.

(7) Comprehensive globalization service

As discussed in Chapter 5, language support is likely to be increasingly incorporated into overall globalization strategies through language management. This trend changes the dynamics of translation from an isolated task to an integrated part of global communication. Merits of this approach also include the application of an internationalization process, which is instrumental to an efficient use of language support as discussed above.

By focusing on new aspects emerging from the new environments, we have now examined teletranslation from the point of view of both the user and the provider. In the following section, teletranslation is observed in relation to Translation-mediated Communication (TMC) in order to highlight further the changes taking place compared with the traditional form of translation.

Translation-mediated Communication with Teletranslation

We have already introduced the concept of TMC in association with CMC (Computer-mediated Communication). In the simplest way, CMC can be depicted as a mode of communication with a computer placed between the Sender and the Receiver carrying the Message. In Chapter 4 we studied CMC in relation to TMC, and highlighted certain aspects that are new to traditional TMC which is based on asynchronous text. From the language support users' perspective, while participating in CMC they may initially be familiar only with traditional communication modes such as face-to-face interactions or communication based on telephone, telegraph, fax and the postal system. Their experience with these channels influences how well they accept, appropriate or adapt themselves to CMC. Once they have become comfortable with CMC, they create new behaviors, some of which resemble earlier ones, e.g. voice chat somewhat resembles conference calls, but has the unique addition of a text chat window. These new channels affect communications behavior in several ways. For example e-mail and chat tend to become more casual and informal than conventional snail mail and face-to-face or phone conversations. This is attributable in part to the absence of eye contact, resulting in a diminishing of face threatening acts (see Brown & Levinson, 1987). In other words, the computer may serve as a channel for exchanging messages, and will also shape the communications behavior of the participants.

However, CMC is not primarily concerned with whether or not there is a common language shared between the Sender and the Receiver, or what language the Message is in. TMC adds these factors to CMC. Providing multilingual support for CMC thus opens new dimensions. The Message subject to TMC now includes multimedia, Web sites or text chat. This shift from analog and atomic environments to digital and virtual communications is creating teletranslation. One of the consequences of this is the change in the nature of the Message that is submitted for translation. Whereas conventional translation was most concerned with the Content, which is a verbal (textual) component of the Message, the Message created in the digital environment has come to require that both the Content and the Package (the non-verbal or non-textual component) are subject to translation.

Even in traditional translation, the Package has always been part of the translation effort, but it tended to be an implicit rather than an explicit element. For example, the type of paper on which a business card is printed may have influenced the Translator who undertook to translate the card but, if it has, it will only have made an implicit impact on the resultant translation. In other words, the Packaging part for translation has generally been at best an implicit element for the translator to manipulate and express into his or her translation outcome. This aspect is even more likely to be strongly manifested in immersive virtual reality environments where nonverbal communication could take place in a fully controllable environment. We will touch on this aspect in our final chapter.

The following section deals with a number of key issues that need to be addressed in working towards the mature teletranslation industry.

Key issues

The observation of teletranslation as it is today suggests a number of questions for its further developments. These issues are discussed from the perspective of both the user and the provider. For the former the goal is to become global-ready and for the latter it is to facilitate that process.

It appears that, as the globalization trend accelerates on the back of the Internet-based infrastructure, organizations are required to become ready for multilingual and multicultural environments in various communication modes. In a future global information society, TMC will likely become an essential integrated component of organizational communication. This will mean that TMC needs to be incorporated into the organization's globalization strategies. Some have already taken this path by employing language management or extensive internationalization practice, for example, but it needs to become widespread practice and further integrated into the organizational communication practice as a whole. The concept of *foundational multilinguality* (Joscelyne, 2000) common in certain international organizations suggests one direction. For the Recipient whose linguistic and cultural conditions are different from those of the Sender, this primarily means consideration of the Message at the authoring stage (in our digital content lifecycle).

Joscelyne (2000) points out further that in international organizations such as OECD translators are regarded as contributing to the 'knowledge-producing chain,' whereas in organizations with no understanding of foundational multilinguality, translation is treated as only subordinate to this chain. Figure 6.2 illustrates these ideas in diagrams adapted from Joscelyne (2000: 87).

In A in Figure 6.2, the authoring stage is in collaboration with language support, which takes Receiver conditions into consideration. The resulting Message is therefore localization- and translation-ready, facilitating the

A An organization with TMC perspective

B An organization without TMC perspective

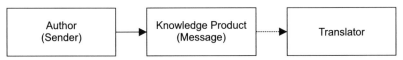

Figure 6.2 Language support as knowledge creation, modified from Joscelyne (2000: 87).

ensuing translation process smoothly. Furthermore, the Translator is perceived to be contributing to knowledge creation. We therefore consider this model to be organizational communication with a TMC perspective. By comparison, B illustrates the situation in which the Message is created without the Receiver's perspective, and therefore the Translator's task becomes more constrained and is not regarded as contributing to knowledge creation. As we have observed, some organizations are moving into pattern A thinking, whereas most organizations remain in the old-fashioned way with pattern B. From the provider's side, teletranslation will increasingly be required to cater to knowledge creation by way of internationalization according to the organization's language management, thus providing a high value-added service. This in turn will impact on the translation communication system to incorporate collaborative authoring with the Sender, which may sometimes even involve consultation with the Receiver. With this in mind, a Translation Communication System (see Figure 2.4) can be envisaged as changing to a Teletranslation Communication System (Figure 6.3).

Figure 6.3 illustrates how the teletranslation processing function is extended to M1 by way of internationalization or in some other consultative manner. This process may sometimes involve the Receiver, as shown by a dotted line in the figure. Also storage and processing functions are linked in cases such as TM tools, which may sometimes be accessed by the Sender as well. With increasingly seamless functionality of communication systems in terms of storage, transmission and processing, teletranslation systems will likely see these functions gradually converge. Processing and storage functionality are already converging in TM (see Chapter 3).

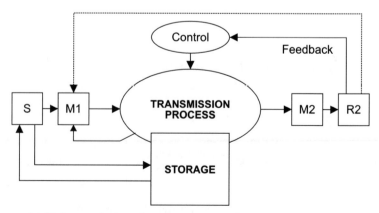

Figure. 6.3 Teletranslation Communication System

Similarly, the transmission mechanism may also become transparent with 'always-on' access to the Internet, as is already the case with wireless communication and is likely to be extended to other communication systems in the future.

This direction also seems to fit in with the new Application Service Provider (ASP) model we mentioned in Chapter 3 (also see Esselink, 2000b). This is a concept of an ASP company putting a robust language management infrastructure in place so that the user organization can plug in its language service providers according to this software-based infrastructure. This can be considered as a model in which the user organization implements a skeleton Teletranslation Communication System through which a chosen language service provider supplies the service. In this scenario, high-tech freelance translators may thrive, since the client already has an infrastructure in place.

In this chapter we have further extended the original concept of teletranslation and observed and interpreted its current direction. The next chapter looks into the possibility of teleinterpretation.

Topics for Further Research or Discussion

(1) As a review of the concepts in this chapter, consider (and describe) what would be involved if a worldwide (gift) flower-distributing company decided to go global. How could it guarantee that it would reach all markets? How would it conceptualize its products (bouquets, message cards, etc.)? Which market locales might not be of high priority? What should the message look like when directed to France, the US, Chile, Taiwan, Japan, Korea?

(2) What would a built-in TMC system look like? (How) could one design a TMC 'product' that could be integrated into a new global company?

Chapter 7

Teleinterpretation

In contrast with translation, which facilitates asynchronous text-based communication, interpretation in its traditional mode deals with synchronous speech-based interactions. This fundamental difference in the mode of communication that interpretation and translation facilitate has meant a delay of the former to develop into teleinterpretation. The Internet has so far favored text-based mode, and voice communication has not advanced to the same extent. In this chapter, we will define teleinterpretation, and examine the current status of remote interpreting as a precursor to teleinterpretation. We will then attempt to describe the paradigm of teleinterpretation in terms of its technical requirements, and address critical issues concerning feasibility of teleinterpretation.

Development of Remote Interpreting

Interpretation as a whole is still largely a synchronous service, based on physical presence that facilitates face-to-face voice communication. However, exceptions exist, such as in the case of remote interpreting. The 1970s saw the beginnings of videoconferencing, followed by early experiments by UNESCO in 1976 and the UN in 1978 on multilingual videoconferencing using satellite links (Mouzourakis, 1996). More recently, feedback from interpreters who have worked in videoconferencing situations seems to be generally negative, mainly due to the insufficient quality of sound and picture (Day, 1996; Mouzourakis, 1996). Although actual instances of interpreting used for videoconferencing as yet are rare, the increasing awareness of this emerging communication mode and its implication for interpretation are apparent in interpretation guidelines issued by AIIC (the International Association of Conference Interpreters) as well as in the CEC (Commission of the European Communities) publication that specifies the requirements for interpretation for videoconferencing (Moser-Mercer, 1997).

Prior to videoconferencing, remote interpreting existed in the form of 'media interpreting' which emerged with the need for simultaneous interpretation for live TV broadcasts; early examples included interpretation for the Apollo 11 mission in 1969, and the Eurikon experiment to test the potential appeal of a European program for satellite TV (Kurz, 1996). This field is expanding today in response to the increasing media coverage of the world and the convergence of broadcasting and IT, with accompanying requirements for language facilitation. However, media interpreting remained largely based on physical transportation rather than on telecommunications in the sense that interpreters would typically travel to the studio where interpretation took place, although normally not to the location of the speaking parties. Associated with media language facilitation is screen translation involving subtitling and dubbing for audiovisual media, which takes place separately from the original production. Until recently, these tasks have also remained location-dependent. In Japan pilot experiments were conducted in 1997 to allow subtitlers to telework using computer and ISDN (Integrated Services Digital Network) connections (JCTV implementing translation, 1997) and similar practices have now been adopted worldwide.

In 1973 the Australian government set up the Emergency Telephone Interpreter Service on a 24-hour basis (Ozolins, 1991). This service was targeted at immigrants in emergency situations and is considered to be the most original contribution to interpreting services in Australia. Between the 1980s and the early 1990s the world's leading telecommunications companies introduced telephone interpretation on a commercial basis. Japan's KDD set up KDD Teleserve in 1986 and the US-based AT&T Language Line was established as a subsidiary of AT&T in 1990, both in order to make interpreting services available on the telephone (O'Hagan, 1996). These services made a certain type of interpretation location-independent as they allowed one to be linked to an interpreter on the telephone.

In order to illustrate how remote interpreting is linked to various types of teleconferencing, Table 7.1 shows the main types of remote conferencing to which remote interpreting may be applied.

According to whether or not it involves only an audio stream or audio plus video streams, 'teleconference' can be classified as audioconference or videoconference. Audioconference, normally known as 'conference calls', link three or more parties concurrently. This is a common form in which telephone interpreting takes place by an interpreter relaying conversation between two parties who are in separate locations. For group-to-group as opposed to one-to-one audioconferencing, a loudspeaking telephone may be used where multiple parties are residing in one location. Videoconference can be categorized depending on various setups. Studio-based or room-based conferencing is the highest-end service and involves dedicated studios or rooms in separate locations linked by audio and video connections. 'Videotelephony' uses dedicated videophone units that convey speech and facial images of the speakers. This concept has not been widely adopted, and instances of remote interpreting do not seem to have

Table 7.1 Teleconference modes in view of remote interpreting

Teleconference Modes	
Type	*Description*
Audio Conference	voice only (conference call)
Video Conference	voice and facial images (video telephony)
	voice and moving images (studio- or room-based)
Audiographic Conference	voice with text and other visuals
Computer Conference	text chat sometimes combined with voice chat, including dynamic links to Web
	moving images in addition to above

been substantiated in this mode. 'Audiographic conferencing' uses two telephone lines, one for voice and the other for data transmission. It is normally equipped with a video display unit linked to a PC, which is used as a common whiteboard that all participants can see and add to. The screen can also be used to display still pictures, as well as text or drawings. This is now advanced to allow collaborative working environments such as shared PowerPoint™ presentations, and may use the Internet for the data transmission. In this way, it is merging with 'computer conferencing', which initially meant text chat, but today often uses voice chat, which normally includes text chat capabilities (see Chapter 4). It is also possible for all the participants to jump to Web sites while communicating via voice. Multimedia desktop conferencing may be best known, with such applications as CUSeeme™ in which a small camera sits on top of each PC, conveying moving images while participants are able to communicate via text chat and/or voice.

Wherever any of the above modes of conferencing takes place between parties who do not share a common language, language facilitation will be required. The next section examines telephone interpreting as a well-established remote mode of interpreting.

Telephone interpreting

The introduction of telephone interpreting seems to reflect different needs that come from different social conditions in each country. For example, in Australia it was based on the needs of its large immigrant population, whereas in Japan the major use of such services has been to facilitate the Japanese making outbound international telephone calls (O'Hagan, 1996). A background similar to that of Australia seems to apply to the USA, where telephone interpreting is used domestically by its immigrants for purposes such as medical interpreting (Hornberger *et al.*, 1996). A significant advantage of combining telephone and interpreting services is summarized by Ozolins:

> With all the inherent drawbacks of communication by telephone, it was nevertheless a most effective way of getting language services in situations where it might have been impossible to provide an interpreter in person, and a most efficient way of handling brief interpreting situations or multilingual information situations, where many calls crossed the boundaries of interpreting/information. (Ozolins, 1991)

The fundamental difference between telephone interpreting and other types of remote interpreting such as videoconference interpreting lies in the fact that telephone interpreting uses telecommunication as a medium to make an interpreting service available without the interpreter being present in person. For example, medical interpreting is typically used by a doctor and a patient who are meeting face-to-face but are not able to communicate because of language barriers. The situation in which remote interpreting may occur can be categorized as follows:

(1) The Sender and the Receiver are in the same location (face to face) with the interpreter linked via telecommunications.
(2) The interpreter is in the same location with either the Sender or the Receiver but the Sender and the Receiver are in separate locations and linked via telecommunications.
(3) The Sender, the Receiver and the interpreter are each in separate locations and linked via telecommunications.

Telephone interpreting may occur in any of the above situations, whereas videoconference interpreting most typically occurs in situation 2. In this sense, videoconference interpreting is not carried out in truly telecommunication-based form, whereas telephone interpreting in situations 1 and 3 shows the characteristics similar to teleinterpretation where the interpreter is not physically present with either the Sender or the Receiver.

The recent US Court Telephone Interpreting Project provides more insight into the nature of telephone interpreting. It was designed to trial the application of telephone interpreting to court interpreting. Its first system was installed in November 1990 at the district court in Las Cruces, New

Mexico, allowing simultaneous interpretation of court proceedings between Spanish and English over the telephone (Vidal, 1998). According to Vidal, since 1995 three other district court interpreters' offices have been participating in the scheme and in the 1996 fiscal year 402 federal court hearings and 222 off-the-record events were interpreted over the telephone. In addition to the federal court systems, Vidal reports, the National Center for State Courts also launched a telephone interpreting pilot program.

The rationale behind adopting this form of interpreting is justified by the Administration Office on the grounds that it makes the services of qualified court interpreters available in locations that lack such resources, and at substantial cost savings to the courts (Mintz, 1998). Although this argument sounds logical in itself, Vidal points to a real question that needs to be addressed: 'the inherent unreliability of the telephone for meaningful communication of important legal matters,' and stresses the importance of nonverbal communication in judiciary settings. While the use of telephone interpreting is accepted by some court interpreters for 'short proceedings, only where no qualified interpreters are available, only if the equipment is sufficiently sophisticated...' a concern is expressed that 'it is a small step to viewing live interpretation as a luxury the [court] system cannot afford' (Vidal, 1998). In the US, the National Association of Judiciary Interpreters and Translators (NAJIT) is currently assessing this new form of court interpreting, as it regards the development of the new mode as 'one of the most important questions to challenge this profession since its inception two decades ago' (Vidal, 1998).

These developments of remote interpreting suggest that it is now in transition, facing the next more ambitious stage that will include wider applications. In the next section, we will outline the paradigm of teleinterpretation in relation to the technical requirements of various forms of remote interpreting.

Teleinterpretation Paradigm

In view of the variety of remote interpreting currently in operation, and in parallel with the definition of teletranslation, we define teleinterpretation to mean: 'interpretation operated over the Internet, where synchronous language facilitation mainly based on voice mode takes place with the Sender, the Receiver of the Message and the interpreter distributed in separate locations.' This is different from the definition provided by the AIIC for what they call 'teleinterpreting' which is described as: 'interpretation of a multilingual videoconference by interpreters who have a direct view of neither the speaker nor their audience' (see http://www.aiic.net/

ViewPage.cfm/page120.htm). In our use of the term, teleinterpretation means remote interpreting applied specifically to CMC supported on the Internet such as distributed computer conferencing. In particular, the computer conferencing mode on the Internet is normally equipped with a shared virtual environment where the participants can draw, call up a document or carry out text chat interactively. The language facilitation in this environment may therefore include a hybrid mode such as trans-terpreting (see Chapter 4).

The paradigm of teleinterpretation can be defined in terms of a number of technical considerations. Today's telephone interpreting services typically use at least three-way conference-call facilities, sometimes with ISDN lines, to secure the highest possible voice quality at 64 kbps. Although the standard conference-call facilities where all parties hear everybody's voices are sufficient for consecutive interpreting, simultaneous interpreting requires additional facilities. For example, in the US Court Telephone Interpreting Project mentioned above, audioconferencing is set up to allow simultaneous interpreting by using dual telephone lines linked via special equipment as described by Mintz (1998). The interpreter wears a headset with an attached microphone with a toggle switch and is linked to two telephone lines that connect the communicating parties in two separate sites. The interpreter flips the switch to feed his or her spoken output in the target language to the appropriate line, while from the other line the interpreter can hear the input in the source language via the headset. The interpreter's headset has a side-tone suppressor to prevent the interpreter's own voice from coming back through the headset. The interpreters who used the system confirm that it provides sufficient sound quality and that, for brief proceedings, the lack of visual cues does not adversely affect the interpreting performance (Mintz, 1998).

ISO technical standards (ISO 2603) specify that equipment used for simultaneous interpretation must provide linear response in the 125–12500 Hz frequency range (Mouzourakis, 1996). Videoconferencing based on narrowband ISDN (N-ISDN) with H.320 standards limits the audio channel capacity to telephone-quality sound (400–3400 Hz) at best and only for a single line, which clearly is not adequate for simultaneous interpreting. Technical requirements for interpreting for videoconferences concern both voice and image quality. For example, the N-ISDN standards for image quality provide for images that are below broadcast TV standards and also limit the number of participants to not more than six or seven persons, owing to consideration of the ratio of dynamic to static image content. Kremer (1997: 42) from the AIIC comments on the sound quality for simultaneous interpreting for videoconferencing: 'Restricted communication bandwidth makes the task far more tiring than under 'live' conditions, and can lead to an inevitable drop in quality' and suggests that the ideal situation would include 'multiple camera views and individual controls, multi-channel communications ... and other facilities.' However, there is a discrepancy in judging the adequacy of the technology between the interpreter and the participants of videoconferencing, where the latter felt the audio and image quality was good enough but the interpreters in the same environment found the contrary (Mouzourakis, 1996). This clearly illustrates the difference in information-processing demands on the interpreters, as compared with those of the participants.

In comparison with studio-based videoconferencing in N-ISDN environments, current desktop videoconferencing imposes further restrictions in quality. It transmits the data in packet mode under a restricted bandwidth as low as 28.8 kbps, which allows one video window and one audio channel. As far as speech quality is concerned, today's voice platforms based on VOIP (voice over IP) or Internet telephony using a packet-based network generally do not provide sufficient quality for interpreting. Given that Internet telephony was originally developed as a trade-off between quality and significantly reduced price compared with circuit-switched telephone calls, it clearly does not serve to provide a sufficient environment for teleinterpretation – at least in its current form.

Today's audio and video applications for PCs are typically unicast (point-to-point communication). While this allows one-to-many communication, such as sending an e-mail message to multiple recipients, it is not economical when sending graphics or video, which need a high bandwidth. By comparison, multicast provides one-to-many, several-to-many, and many-to-many distribution. However, these are currently described as 'best effort' services because multicast uses only the User Datagram Protocol (UDP) and not the Transport Control Protocol (TCO) of the IP suite (Brutzman, 1997). The key to making multicast feasible on a worldwide scale is considered to be high bandwidth Internet backbone connections and the use of (dedicated) workstations (Brutzman, 1997).

With technological conditions still evolving, a number of open issues require closing before teleinterpretation can be enabled. Given that the Internet is heading towards broadband with the development of Internet II and with the next generation of wireless technology known as 3G (see Chapter 4), it is difficult to predict the exact impact of these advancements on conferencing environments and on remote interpreting. However, it seems quite clear that the issue of nonverbal communication is significant to the development of teleinterpretation and this is the focus of the following section, which further examines teleinterpretation in the context of TMC.

Translation-mediated Communication with Teleinterpretation

The Sender and the Receiver

One major difference between the conventional form of interpretation and teleinterpretation is that in the latter the Sender and the Receiver are in different physical locations. And yet, unlike the conventional form of translation, which has always had the Sender and the Receiver in separate locations, in teleinterpretation all communication parties are linked via a synchronous communication mode. Also, unlike telephone interpreting, the communication space, which the Sender and the Receiver share, allows interactions using text or other visual images in addition to voice. This may mean that the interaction does not have to rely on spoken words alone, since other communication channels are available for visual displays of diagrams or any other images. The virtual sharable environment also means that various channels between the teleinterpreter and the Sender or the Receiver can be used for the purpose of confirming the meaning without disturbing the other party.

Another new aspect of teleinterpretation is in terms of the role of the teleinterpreter as a mediator, as has sometimes been recognized with the interpreter's role in telephone interpreting. Oviatt and Cohen (1992) found that, in telephone interpreting, interpreters assume an independent, managerial role regarding information sequencing, including turn giving. Computer conferencing in CMC often requires a meeting facilitator to adopt such a role and it is easy to imagine that the role of the teleinterpreter would also involve facilitation. In particular, given that the Sender and the Receiver are not able to communicate directly, it will be difficult to establish and enforce protocols of turn taking during the interaction. It will be appropriate, in some cases, for the teleinterpreter to assume the role of mediator, thereby facilitating a smooth flow of TMC.

The Message

While one of the major concerns in teleinterpreting is the lack of nonverbal communication cues available in face-to-face interactions, it seems likely that CMC creates its own way of compensating for the absence of such information. As we discussed in Chapter 4, a crude but effective method based on the use of emoticons or 'emote' commands has been developed in text-based CMC. In most voice chat sessions, it is also possible for the speaker to add nonverbal information in the form of emoticons or via avatar's facial expressions. The study by Oviatt and Cohen (1992) on telephone interpreting points to one direction in compensating for the lack of nonverbal cues in that requests for confirmation amounted to 31.5% of total words in interpreted calls. With the lack of back-channeling (nodding, approving smiles and the like) from the Receiver of the Message, the communicating parties need to have confirmation by way of more explicit verbalization to compensate for the lack of nonverbal cues. This suggests that the way teleinterpretation needs to operate will depend on how people will use CMC in compensating for the lack of nonverbal information.

As far as the current use of emoticons and avatars is concerned, some ambiguity related to nonverbal cues is made more explicit in certain CMC Messages. For example, when the Sender attaches an emoticon such as ;-) (a smiling face with a wink) at the end of somewhat sarcastic comments, the Receiver (and the teleinterpreter) knows that they are said in tongue-in-cheek fashion rather than with real sarcasm. By comparison, in face-to-face interactions, reading the Sender's nonverbal cues is not always clear-cut.

In terms of mode of language facilitation, new characteristics of the Message can be seen in its features to include interactive text chat (see Chapter 4), thus involving transterpreting. It is also possible to present the Message in forms other than verbalized content such as drawings or images to explain certain ideas. The use of virtual whiteboards can stimulate such flexibility. In the same way, the teleinterpreter will be able to use it to convert the verbalized Message into something other than words by drawing a visual image, for example. If the teleinterpreter's role here becomes more of a mediator than strictly as an interpreter, he or she will be able to take more liberty in the way to make the point.

This seems to suggest that whole dynamics among the Sender, the Receiver and the Interpreter changes with teleinterpretation as the platform for communication becomes telecommunication-based and the nature of the Message changes. In the process of establishing teleinterpretation, it also seems likely that some features of translating and interpreting merge. While these are mainly our own speculations, on the basis of our experiments on transterpreting (see Chapter 4) and synchronous instruction provided on the Internet (see Chapter 8), we are able to suggest a number of aspects that are significant in considering the feasibility of teleinterpretation. The next section addresses these issues.

Critical Issues

By comparison with the development of teletranslation, the nature of interpretation has made it far more resistant to shifting to telecommunication-based modes. For example, the attitude of professional bodies of interpreters seems negative towards the use of new media to allow remote interpreting. This illustrates a conflict between new technology applications, often driven by economic factors, and professional practices built on the basis of a set of conditions according to the then-dominant technology – physical transportation in the case of face-to-face interpreting. The AIIC standards for videoconferencing (AIIC Code for the Use of New Technologies in Conference Interpretation: http://www.aiic.net/ViewPage.cfm/page120.htm) where some of the participants are in remote locations, state that 'having a direct view of the entire context of the event where the messages are being interpreted is essential [for the interpreters].' For the cases where interpreters work from off-site the AIIC's position is unequivocally negative:

> The temptation to make certain technologies deviate from their original goal by coming up with the idea, for example, of placing interpreters in front of monitors/screens to interpret from a distance a meeting at which all the participants are gathered in the same location (tele-interpretation) is **unacceptable** [emphasis in the original]. (AIIC)

Given that judiciary interpreting on the telephone means that the interpreter is often the only party communicating off-site, such a practice would be out of the question according to the above standard. Nevertheless, the speed at which the technology is advancing suggests that 'the interpreting process... needs to be explored in light of new working conditions in the "virtual" world' (Moser-Mercer, 1997: 195). Vidal (1998) also admits that 'as telecommunications technology advances in the next few years, live interpreters will become the exception rather than the norm'. Indications are that the interpreting profession is faced with a new challenge, which comes from infrastructural changes increasingly allowing sophisticated forms of CMC, thus pointing to the possibility of teleinterpretation. In this section, two issues are addressed in terms of needs arising from CMC on the Internet, and also the role that various nonverbal communication cues play in the practice of interpreting.

Characteristics of CMC on the Internet

A fundamental change in thinking is necessary for considering teleinterpretation in terms of the user needs. It therefore seems to be exactly the wrong direction to regard teleinterpretation as a matter of transferring today's interpretation function onto the Internet. Such mistakes have been made, for example, in the field of education with Web-based learning where the same materials that the teacher would use in face-to-face class are transferred on the Web and are taught more or less in the same way as in the physical classroom. Both what the learner seeks and the way in which the teacher responds to the learner's need are often different on the Internet from face-to-face interactions (Palloff & Pratt, 1999). Similarly, virtual meetings in CMC where interpretation is called upon will be somewhat different from meetings that take place face to face, at least until such time as technology enables a virtual meeting environment that is indistinguishable from a physical meeting.

Schrage (1990) sees one direction of technology developments as creating an infrastructure that supports productive collaboration. The authors can attest that the Internet provides such a function on the basis that for a number years we have worked jointly reliant on CMC where e-mail, text chat and VOIP have all contributed to our work in collaboration. It is difficult to measure how much difference it might have made if we had had regular face-to-face meetings, but our feeling is that such meetings may not have made a considerable difference, if any. In this way, CMC may develop at least initially as a way to facilitate collaborative work by increasingly allowing real-time interactions in digital environments that are in some context superior to the atomic environments of face-to-face meetings. For example, people having a discussion in a computer conferencing environment will be able to call up a related document on screen, or to draw or show an image during the discussion as required. The same degree of flexibility in accessing various pieces of information synchronously may not always be possible with in-person meetings. As Schrage points out, effective cross-cultural collaboration using technology is a global phenomenon, and this is the context into which teleinterpretation has to fit. In such an environment, interpreters may find the motivations of the communicating parties different from physical meetings. For example, mutual exploration of new ideas and confirmation of mutual understanding may be strong features, rather than consensus seeking on pre-determined issues.

On the basis of our experiment on transterpreting, the nature of the language facilitation is most likely to be multitasking, and also hybrid between translating and interpreting. In this environment, interpreting (being intended for synchronous communication) may be more applicable than translating. At the same time, the conventional distinction between translation as text-based and interpretation as voice-only will likely become blurred since asynchronous and synchronous communication modes are merging. For example, it is possible to attach voice messages to one's e-mail. In this way, the nature of CMC will be different from the familiar conventional characteristics of the Message that the translator and the interpreter have been processing. In particular, CMC highlights the role of nonverbal information for its virtue of not having appropriate channels. This is a significant issue in interpreting as we discuss below.

The role of nonverbal communication in interpreting

Auditory information is obviously critical to any mode of interpretation, and it has been experimentally proven that the noise factor of the transmission system is directly linked to interpreter performance (De Groot, 1997). Furthermore, unlike text-based translation, interpreting practice founded on face-to-face interactions ideally demands multimodality in the transmission function. Viaggio (1997a, 1997b) suggests that nonverbal communication is inherently part of the interpreting process as it deals with speech mostly in face-to-face situations. Viaggio maintains, however, that despite its significance this aspect has often been neglected in interpreting. It is rather ironic that the attention to nonverbal communication elements in interpretation seems to have been highlighted by the introduction of new modes of communication that cut off such nonverbal communication (Massaro & Moser-Mercer, 1996).

In face-to-face interpreting environments, the interpreter imparts the intended meaning of the Sender by combining the nonverbal and verbal elements of the Message in the source language into a verbal rendition in the target language. However, it is extremely difficult to quantify just how much information is conveyed by nonverbal cues, particularly given that in both intra and inter-lingual communication such nonverbal cues are not always consciously produced or received (Argyle, 1988). In the context of interpreting, videoconferencing has often been accused of losing such cues, thus straining the interpreter's concentration (Kremer, 1997). On the other hand, there is a report (Mintz, 1998) that telephone interpreting is better in terms of concentration on the Message without any distraction from other channels that may be presented to the interpreter. There is a similar report on the positive aspect of not having the moving image of the speaker in educational settings on the Internet, as such images tend to distract the participants (Palloff & Pratt, 1999).

One unique aspect of nonverbal communication specific to interpretation is the fact that, when interpretation is delivered, the interpreter may use some nonverbal cues that may or may not be seen by the Receiver owing to the constraints of the room setting, as is often the case with simultaneous interpreting, where the interpreter is not in the direct view of the Receivers. Furthermore, as a rule, interpreters do not attempt to reproduce the speaker's nonverbal cues such as kinesics (body movements) or facial expressions. At the same time, aspects of the Sender's nonverbal cues will be conveyed unmodified to the Receiver for whom it could potentially lead to a visual and auditory mismatch. For example, in a typical conference-interpreting situation, the audience hears the interpreter's voice through the earphone, but is seeing the Sender's kinesics instead of the inter-preter's. An animated speech given by a Spanish speaker may be deliber-ately toned down by the interpreter for an English audience who expects a more sedate speech delivery, but nevertheless the speaker's kinesics are observed by the audience.

In summary, two problems exist for teleinterpretation: (1) bandwidth issues, and (2) methods of managing communication between tele-interpreter and the other parties to the communication. The second issue grows in complexity if we consider future situations that involve immer-sive virtual reality such as HyperReality (see Chapter 10). Another current problem is the lack of familiarity of conventional interpreters with the tele-communication environments that may be used for interpreting, and the need to adapt to situations that have not arisen in conventional inter-preting. The standards for interpreters developed by AIIC appear to be a case of judging future developments with the 'rear-view mirror' in a sense that they strictly define the existing environments for interpretation, and motivate against the kinds of flexibility that are required in the Internet environment. Of course, the number and kinds of channels of communica-tion that one finds in face-to-face interaction are more limited in the Internet environment, although new channels also develop. In particular, various types of nonverbal communication are not present on the Internet, and the methods of compensating for these types are not well developed. The individual communicator naturally cannot develop unconscious nonverbal communication behavior, since the person is by definition unaware of several types of communication that he or she is using. Whether and how unconscious nonverbal communication affects interpre-tation are open questions.

The question of teleinterpretation illustrates the undefined nature of the future developments we are discussing. As an interim conclusion, we can say that a teleinterpreter must be able to combine the skills of the telephone interpreter (no visual context) with the ability to carry out sight translation and, until the bandwidth improves, may have to establish a protocol that allows the interpreter more managerial license (as in the case of the tele-phone interpreter described above). That is, the new context for inter-preting requires a new, flexible attitude and a set of skills that already exist, but are used in conventional contexts in different ways. This is yet another reason why education to prepare translators and interpreters for future possibilities is critical. In the next chapter we will look at virtual learning environments that are developing for translators and interpreters.

Topics for Further Research or Discussion

(1) In working with computers, 'multitasking' refers to using more than one application at a time, e.g. translating a text while keeping open and consulting online glossaries and communicating by text chat with fellow translators about a translation problem. Interpreters multitask in conventional interpreting because they are listening to one language and speaking in another almost simultaneously, and may also be trying to perform such tasks as number conversion – necessary especially in languages such Chinese, which has a unit of 10,000 (*wan*) such that 'twenty thousand' is 'two ten thousands' (two *wan*). Given that teleinterpreting will involve using a computer and a desktop, with more than one communication channel available, what do you think a teleinterpreter's workstation would include? What tasks would they be likely to perform?

(2) For your language combination, what aspects of nonverbal communication in the source language are likely to pose problems in communicating in the target language? In using teleinterpreting, (how) is it possible to overcome these problems?

Chapter 8
Virtual Communities for Translators and Interpreters

With the last two chapters we have examined teletranslation and tele-interpretation, focusing on the practical dimensions involved in their operation. As such, we have addressed the needs of Translation providers and to some extent those of users. In this chapter, we switch our attention to Translation education. This chapter draws on our experiences in both teaching and attending virtual courses on Translation in order to examine the possibility of the Internet as a place for professional development for translators and interpreters.

Internet-based Learning for Translators

We have so far outlined the emerging practice of Translation as teletranslation and teleinterpretation. The profession of Translation is undergoing a significant change, requiring the practitioners to obtain new knowledge and skills. The gap between supply and demand in human resources proficient to work in such new fields as localization seems to be widening. The need to address this issue is clearly illustrated in the recent efforts of the LISA Education Initiative Taskforce (LEIT) launched in 1998 and the Certified Localization Professional (CLIP) also commenced in 1998 by the Irish Software Localization Interest Group to bring industry and educational institutions together to respond to the market demand. Similarly, the Language Engineering for Translators Curricula (LETRAC) project by the European Commission has been designed to introduce curricula suitable for today and for future Translation market requirements. Its rationale is explained as:

> Industrial companies are using sophisticated software and tools in all areas of document creation, terminology management and translation. Changes in these commercial environments have not yet been fully reflected in the training of translators and technical writers who need to develop appropriate skills and knowledge in information technology (IT) to match the environments of their major prospective employers. (LETRAC, 1998)

LETRAC's analysis of the current situation in IT training for language professionals is described as 'arbitrary,' where such courses on terminology management and text processing may be provided, but mostly in a piecemeal and non-systematic manner. LETRAC is designed to incorporate IT skills and knowledge of language engineering into the existing translator and interpreter training programs throughout the translation and interpretation departments of European universities. One of the criticisms of LETRAC, however, is that it is 'so extensive, that one wonders when the students would have time to actually translate' (Inggs, 2000). There have been various discussions as to how much emphasis needs to be given to technology in the training of translators (e.g. see Abaitua, 1999) and as yet no conclusive answers appear to have been found. A broad summary of the current situation regarding the need for technology training is that translators and interpreters are more or less left to their own devices to learn new skills and acquire required knowledge. Maia (2000) comments: 'Though many in the translation community cheerfully insist "they can pick it up as they go along" it remains probably true that most people ... would appreciate more formal training in the use of these new forms of technology...'

An on-line symposium *Innovation in Translator and Interpreter Training (ITIT)* held between 17 and 25 January 2000 was organized by the Intercultural Studies Group at the Universitat Rivira I Virgili, Tarragona, Spain with a similar impetus to address the current situation in which 'changing labor markets mean it is no longer sufficient to maintain traditional standards' in the training of translators and interpreters. This applies to both new and potential translators and interpreters and also to practicing professionals, as observed by Torres del Rey (2000): 'As the vertiginous development of technology demands constant self-adjustment, continuing education is more and more necessary.' To this end, he further suggests as a method of delivery for such professional developments that: 'Distance learning is increasingly becoming an option for today's world...'

A number of university-based distance-mode courses are offered on the Internet, as in the case of City University in London for the Postgraduate Certificate in Translation Skills (Connell, 1999), New York University School of Continuing and Professional Studies, and University of Hawaii at Manoa Outreach College (O'Hagan, 1999), which we will examine more in detail as a case study below. It seems that the Internet provides an ideal opportunity to deliver professional courses for translators and interpreters that will facilitate their transition to newly emerging working environments. However, how do these courses differ from their traditional counterparts of face-to-face attendance-based and paper- and audio tape-based correspondence courses? On the basis of the authors' experience, the following case studies describe advantages and shortcomings of virtual courses.

Web-based Course: Case Study 1

Introduction

The University of Hawaii at Manoa Outreach College offers totally Web-based non-credit Translation Techniques courses for English/Chinese and English/Japanese. This case study is based on the second installment of the course, which started in September 1999 for the duration of 11 weeks (the first installment was April 1999). Ashworth (one of the authors), the course supervisor, summarized the rationale of the course as: 'The Web is becoming the locus for much of the work in translation, and work on the Web involves the cultivation of Web literacy and use of Web resources' (O'Hagan, 1999). To this end, the course was designed to help improve the skills of mainly practicing translators who wish to work in the Internet environment with the emphasis on the following aspects:

- recognizing translation problems and finding solutions;
- using Web translation skills to transmit translations via Internet/Web;
- practicing translation quality control;
- assessing translation;
- working as a team on the Internet.

The applicants for the course need to sit screening tests for bi-directional translation for the respective language pair (i.e. English to Chinese and Chinese to English, and the same for English and Japanese). The tests are carried out online through the course Web site, whereby the clock starts ticking as soon as the candidate opens the test page. This requirement also discourages those who do not have Web access in either Chinese or Japanese. The staff teaching the course are from the Center for Interpretation and Translation Studies (CITS) at the University of Hawaii, which also provides attendance-based courses for translation and interpretation in Chinese, Japanese and Korean. The unique features of this Web-based course included:

(1)   it involves languages with non-ASCII character sets that are normally more challenging for online communications than their ASCII counterparts in terms of electronic transmission and processing of text;

(2)   the fee is affordable to most freelance and in-house translators as well as full-time students;

(3)   the course attracts students from truly global locations as it is entirely Web-based.

Global classroom

The first course assignment of self-introduction provided the participants with a taste of the global classroom, as postings came from wide geographical locations, including Australia, Japan, New Zealand, Taiwan, the UK and the US (both mainland and Hawaii) for participants in both Chinese and Japanese tracks. The students were divided into two separate tracks, although their paths converged from time to time for exercises that used English texts as a common source for both languages. The participants included both aspiring translators and practicing professionals who nevertheless had little formal training before. The course provider attributed the initial success of this non-credit course in maintaining a high continuation rate of participation to its being aimed primarily at professional training rather than academic credit.

Proof of the need for this type of portable globally-accessible course operated entirely on the Web is evident from the growth in the enrolment numbers from 11 students for the first installment to 20 for the current intake. The geographical distribution of the participants illustrated the different charging systems for the use of telecommunications. For example, people accessing the course from Japan expressed their concern about the high telecommunication costs, which they may incur during the course. Unlike in the USA, New Zealand or Australia where local calls are free or of nominal cost, in Japan subscribers are charged per minute for local calls or access to the Internet.

Course contents

The course assumes that the participants are reasonably familiar with the Internet/Web and are able to access suggested resources as well as read/send messages in/to appropriate forums, which were set up in the course's Bulletin Board system (see Figure 8.1). The course calendar shows the timetable and the appropriate Web page for retrieving assignments and related information. During the course the students are also required to subscribe to an appropriate language-specific translators' mailing list, through which they are expected to solve some of the translation problems.

The course is practically oriented in that participants are set translation tasks of the texts selected mainly from various Web resources. The selected texts for analysis and translation are all real-world and topical subjects, ranging from birth certificates to semi-technical writing and documents related to newly-released software. Prior to translation, each participant is required to analyze the source text (by initially paraphrasing it in his or her native language) in order to identify any particular problems. Translation tasks are carried out into both native and non-native language, although individual students are required to translate for the most part into their native language. The assignments are posted to a designated bulletin board forum through which all students are able to view other participants' translations. Translations are in turn peer reviewed according to pre-determined criteria, and each participant must incorporate the comments received from an assigned reviewer.

The course also includes a few sessions on group-based translation tasks. Each participant is allocated into a small group of people with whom translation assignments must be carried out. Given that people in the team are complete strangers and that all participants are in geographically separate locations, this gives a taste of working in a virtual team, which will be a commonplace for teletranslation. The students are required to submit assignments each week via a designated bulletin board site on the Web, and the time of submission is automatically recorded. The final assignment includes the presentation of a translation log (called a 'protocol') to record the entire translation process with each student observing him or herself through a particular translation assignment.

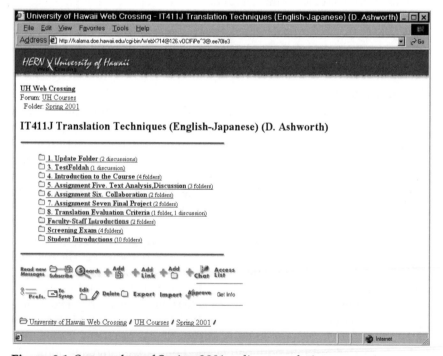

Figure 8.1 Screen shot of Spring 2001 online translation course

In terms of online and offline time required to be spent by the students, the translation tasks themselves are carried out offline, whereas the reading of fellow students' messages may take place online. Real-time chat components were considered, but the time differences between the regions represented by the participants made synchronous communication practically impossible. In terms of future developments, the use of simulations of time-intensive tasks, such as translating investment newsletters with a deadline, is being considered as a means of both taking advantage of the online environment and illustrating the kinds of skills one needs to operate under pressure.

Student–instructor dichotomy

The course provider explains that the teacher–student ratio is no different from the face-to-face counterpart course and that the instructors are there primarily as facilitators. However, on the basis of experience gained from the initial course, the present course has been designed to include more interactions among students partly to nurture the sense of community and partly to reduce the previously excessive workload experienced by the instructors. To illustrate the point, by the first three weeks into the course the number of messages posted (mainly assignments, but including notices from instructors) had exceeded 300. Although not all messages are relevant to all instructors (as some are for Japanese-only and others for Chinese), the quantity is indicative of the considerable time that instructors must allocate to facilitation. This time-consuming aspect of dealing with messages in virtual courses is also pointed out by Connell (1999) based on his experience with offering translation courses on the Internet at the City University in London. Because practically all interactions are in written form (e-mail messages), this could make online courses much more onerous than equivalent face-to-face instruction from the instructor's perspective. This may suggest that online courses require a lower student ratio per teacher. From the student's perspective, it is important that their messages are at least acknowledged. Unless this process is kept up, the student will experience the negative aspect of distance learning in comparison with face-to-face classes. In terms of preparation of the materials, it is also obvious that considerable time was spent finding appropriate and current contents and assembling them into hypertext format.

In comparison with the traditional extramural course, online courses offer immediacy of communication in the same sense as electronic mail. Other advantages outlined by Ashworth (O'Hagan, 1999) include: (1) flexible time factor where students can log in at any time convenient for them; (2) students can work at their own pace within reasonable time constraints, and (3) the opportunity to draw on resources such as fellow students from many different locations, and mailing lists. The current (Summer 2001) course also allows the student to use HTML in composing some of their on-line communications, e.g. in Web Crossing, the asynchronous bulletin board system being used for the current sessions.

Insights gained

A number of unique aspects of the distance-learning mode for transla-tors on the Internet emerged from the perspectives of both the provider and the receiver of the above course:

A sense of virtual community

The main difference between conventional classroom learning and conventional postal-based distance learning lies in the lack of interactions among learners in the latter. While the lack of social interactions in online courses has not been found to be a significant drawback for effective learning, learners nevertheless seek such interactions to make learning more enjoyable. The above course was cognizant of the problem of lack of social interactions, and tried to overcome it. For example, the first session was devoted to self-introductions, whereby each participant posted his or her own introduction to which others were asked to respond. Fostering a sense of community will also affect any subsequent group activities, such as translating in teams and peer feedback.

In order for any virtual learning based on the online environment to be effective, building up a sense of community seems to be a significant factor. Rheingold (1995) developed a concept of 'virtual communities', which are ephemeral in the sense of the physical substance of the community, but are bound on the basis of common interests of the people who participate in the community. He describes the virtual community as a cognitive and social place, not a geographic one, and yet the community spirit can be just as strong as in a physical community. In online learning environments, there is a clear commonality across learners in terms of the interest in the given subject. To foster this aspect, it is essential for the course to provide a common posting place such as a mailing list or bulletin board system or a chat room.

Global perspectives

One distinctive advantage of online courses as compared with face-to-face courses is the tendency of the former to attract participants from a wide range of geographical locations. For example, the participants for the Japanese track of the above course were a mixture of those resident in Japan and those resident elsewhere, although they were all translating between

English and Japanese. This offered the possibility for learners to make contacts and interact with fellow learners in the same professional field who are operating across different parts of the world. For the real work situation with translation, having team members scattered in different geographical locations is also becoming a realistic situation. Thus, providing an international classroom seems appropriate, and is even increasingly a necessary factor.

Having international participants also means that in-country translators (those who live in the target-language country) and their out-of-country counterparts can complement each other's skills and learn from one another. One of the unique advantages that online translation training can provide is the possibility of providing advanced language instruction to individuals who are no longer residing in their native country, but wish to remain current in the use of their language ('native language maintenance'). They can do so by participating in translation courses, where they will acquire two types of knowledge: updating of current knowledge of native language, and enhanced translation skills. Similarly, in-country translators may subscribe to the courses to enhance their source language skills.

Peer feedback and peer interactions (virtual team)

Related to the above issue is the benefit of peer feedback. Unlike paper-based and post-based correspondence courses, Web-based platforms allow productive peer feedback mechanisms with a well-designed structure. As mentioned earlier, working in a virtual team is increasingly a reality, and translators and interpreters need to be able to function effectively in such an environment. The nature of the Internet means that it provides a suitable environment for learners to see one another's work and make comments. However, a drawback may be that the lack of face-to-face encounters may lead to misunderstandings where suggestions for improvements can be taken negatively by the recipient (Palloff & Pratt, 1999). In this sense, one needs to be aware of the fact that the Internet used primarily as a text medium, as it is today, neglects certain communication aspects, such as nonverbal cues. Cases of virtual vandalism in the form of flaming or spamming have been reported (Tiffin & Rajasingham, 2001). This indicates the somewhat delicate nature of interacting in a virtual environment, of which participants as well as instructors need to become aware.

Student–instructor dynamics

The psychodynamics of interaction in a conventional face-to-face classroom are very complex and depend both on the learner preferences and on the teaching styles of the teacher. Generally, teachers acknowledge that creating a good social environment for learning facilitates instruction, whether it be teacher-fronted or student-driven. The transition from such a conventional (student-driven) environment that tries to take advantage of the social dynamics, presents new problems and opportunities. Generally, we believe that teachers of online courses would agree, following Kiraly (2000b), that it is desirable to create an optimum environment for sociocultural learning. The difficulty in online courses is exacerbated by the lack of immediate feedback of the type one can get in face-to-face interaction. Inadequate Web literacy, including the knowledge of how to use CMC, is another compounding factor as discussed below.

Flexibility in delivery to fit working learner requirements

For professional training courses, learners are often full-time workers. Web-based learning environments provide the flexibility to carry on studies without being bound to a particular place (classroom) at a particular time, although certain deadlines will need to be met for assignments. This also relates to an approach that is more learner-centered than teacher-centered. The increasing number of flexible learning courses on the Internet will mean that translators who are keen to develop skills will be given a wider range of opportunities, even if they do not live in a university town or in a city where appropriate courses are offered. Virtual learning is a rapidly expanding area and yet, in the context of translator and interpreter training, we have yet to see well-defined requirements for establishing such courses. In particular, there seems to be a paucity of online courses for interpreters. We will come back to this issue later in this chapter.

Internet and CMC literacy

A problem arises when learners with a minimum level of familiarity with the Internet environment take an online course and the instructor assumes that the students will somehow pick up the skills of using CMC and other necessary facilities on their own. The instructor soon learns to his or her dismay that many learners still need help. If such help (even if it is only an option) is not built into the design of the course, the instructor will have to spend considerable time not only providing help, but also getting students to go online and use the tools available to them, thus causing an enormous distraction from subject teaching.

The next section discusses a pilot Teletranslation and Teleinterpretation course that we conducted on the Internet between September and November 2000.

Web-based Course: Case Study 2

Introduction

The Global Virtual University (GVU) was based on the vision and concept of Professor Emeritus John Tiffin (Tiffin & Rajasingham, 1995) with the overall objective of preparing learners for the emerging information society. In doing so, its aim is to be able to remove the geographical obstacles and allow learners to pursue their interests in particular areas of study. One of the major features of the GVU is its use of synchronous communications mode to deliver real-time interactive lectures on the Internet. In particular, to enable access by learners with a wide range of computing and communication environments, GVU deliberately chooses to use a commercially popular VOIP (voice over IP) platform rather than a high-end proprietary system. This means that students with varying degrees of computer literacy will find it relatively easily to create a voice-enabled environment on their computers. For its pilot courses, the GVU used Hearme™, which was one of the popular voice platforms at the time. With this technology, students who registered for the course were given a password to the GVU site from which they could download the client software free of charge. The GVU also provided technical support that allowed students to test the software before the course started to ensure it was working to the expected level.

The GVU hosted our 10-week Teletranslation and Teleinterpretation pilot course, developed by the authors, with the main objective of testing the voice technology for the purpose of providing instruction to a group of remote students. We also had a secondary objective of exploring both the content, which is new to translators and interpreters, and a particular teaching philosophy. In addition to these objectives, we also had our agenda of evaluating the technology (not necessarily overtly) from the perspective of using it for teleinterpretation. The following section discusses each point that we discovered as a result of the pilot.

VOIP technology

So far most virtual universities have adopted the asynchronous mode of communication primarily using a Web platform, which includes e-mail and a mailing list or bulletin board system. The main reason for most institutions not using a synchronous mode of communication is its unreliability at the current stage of voice technology developments on the Internet. For example, we have found that IP-based voice transmissions are influenced by many variables such as the quality of the telecommunications connection that each student is using, the modem speed and the computer capacity. Any of these factors among any of the students in the group could affect the quality of voice delivery for the entire group. The traffic volume on the Internet at the particular time of our session also greatly influenced the voice quality. Another hindering factor for using a synchronous mode is the practical difficulty of finding a common time slot that suits everyone when a class consists of participants from different parts of the world. In fact, this was the reason why the above Hawaii course did not use real-time chat function. However, the real-time interactive mode, as trialed in the GVU sessions, provides realism and is perhaps more effective in creating a sense of close-knit community among learners and the instructors by allowing them to hear the actual voices of the participants who are otherwise only virtually present.

The voice platform is particularly useful when it is supported by interactive whiteboard functionality that allows the participants to draw a picture, write a short message or call up and display a document for everybody in the group to see in real-time. Another useful feature is the ability for the participants to access a specified Web site during a lecture. For example, with this function the instructor can demonstrate certain features by referring to specified Web sites while providing a voice-based guide to instruct the learners to look at a particular area of the site. It has become clear to us that the voice-based platform on the Internet does not achieve its full potential if it is used only for one-way lectures. Even for lecturing, instructors are best advised to use multimedia functions to retain participants' attention. However, the use of streaming audio and video also has the danger of becoming a 'rear-view mirror' if instructors rely too exclusively on them, e.g. by providing digital audio or video versions of conventional lectures rather than integrating these into the Web environment in effective ways.

One of the important aspects of successfully using a voice platform on the Internet is to establish a speaking protocol among the people attending the course. Hearme™ and other voice platforms have their own ways of indicating who is speaking. For example, Hearme™ displays a list of participants' names with an arrow next to the current speaker's name. However, if anybody wishes to override the present speaker, a protocol is needed to indicate that intention. In our case, people who want to speak next used a chat box to write 'mic please' or an equivalent short message. This was not the most elegant and efficient method, but seemed to work most of the time as long as the present speaker or the moderator notices the signal. Any online course using a real-time voice needs to establish speaking protocols at the beginning of the course. This also means that teaching online therefore involves multitasking in a specific way that is unique to online environments.

The voice communication program that was used in our course had certain inconveniences compared with other voice communication programs. For example, Paltalk™ allows for simultaneous text chat and provides icons for individuals to virtually 'raise their hand' when they wish to take the microphone. By comparison, designing a protocol to indicate 'wish to talk' with Hearme™ is cumbersome, and the text chat feature is also crude. In terms of economic aspects, if an institution wishes to offer courses that involve intensive real-time voice communication, it must acquire a proprietary license to use existing servers and software, which can cost as much as US$100,000.

In summary, although the technology showed enormous potential, our shared feelings were that the current VOIP platforms are not stable enough to use for instruction on a commercial basis, particularly in today's standard narrowband telecommunications environments. For example, during our course we experienced sudden disappearances of voices and numerous access problems. These interruptions often meant that the lecturer needed to repeat the section that the particular participant lost, or start the lecture again. Such inconsistency in the delivery environment was considered as inadequate, and also contributed to extra stress for both the instructor and the learners.

Content

The course was intended to explore new aspects of translation and interpretation, as we have been doing in this book. We felt that the use of the Internet environment for instruction matches well with the particular nature of the course. For example, we were able to demonstrate some of the culturalization aspects of Web localization by actually visiting certain sites while lecturing. The use of a shared whiteboard was also found useful to some extent, although the functionality available in the particular platform we were using was cumbersome. We were also able to try search engines with all participants while the lecturer gave instructions to follow. These activities seemed to be well received by the participants. However, the major disappointment for us was the fact that we were not able to demonstrate teleinterpretation, mainly because of the unstable nature of the voice technology as explained above. For a future pilot, we are also planning to demonstrate or examine in real-time certain translation tools such as Translation Memory (TM) and MT.

As compared with entirely asynchronous courses, real-time lecturing meant that the course needed to be prepared in terms of both asynchronous and synchronous contents. In particular, as in the face-to-face situations, the synchronous contents need to allow certain flexibility to respond to specific interactions with the learners.

Teaching philosophy

We have followed the approach taken by the GVU as a whole, which is in part based on the Vygotskian approach with social constructivist orientation rather than a conventional instructional orientation; the former acknowledges the role of learners in facilitating learning by peers and promotes learner autonomy. In a field as new as teletranslation and teleinterpretation pedagogy, there are many more questions than there are answers, so our approach was more 'ignorance-based' than knowledge-based.

We have become increasingly aware that some of the concepts that we have introduced in this book are not established ideas. It is true to say that we ourselves are still grappling with these concepts with regard to future developments, and it is therefore not possible to teach entirely on the basis of the existing body of knowledge. We have therefore found it useful to make the focus of our teaching ignorance-based by marking gray areas as such. In this approach, the teacher admits his or her ignorance and helps the students to define their own areas of ignorance in order to mutually seek new knowledge. This approach in turn encouraged us to adopt an exploratory and a collaborative style of teaching, which resembles seminar-based interactions. We believe that, once the voice-based platform on the Internet becomes a stable technology, it will provide an appropriate environment to use for this style of teaching.

We have also realized that the ignorance-based approach in turn made the traditional top-down or teacher-centered approach unsuitable (particularly since the teacher himself or herself is admitting his or her ignorance!). We have therefore attempted a learner-centered as opposed to teacher-centered approach. In other words, we have subscribed to a social-constructivist orientation rather than an objectivist approach. Kiraly proposes such a learner-centered approach for translator education:

> ... learning to be a professional translator means learning to act like one. Seen this way, the teacher has no knowledge that the students must or even can acquire – the students will instead have to construct their own knowledge of the profession and their own understandings of their responsibilities and rights as professionals through experience, by collaboratively participating in the authentic activities of professional translators. From such a perspective, the teacher must step down from the distribution pedestal. (Kiraly, 2000b)

As Kiraly has illustrated, it is also essential for the classroom to be part of the 'authentic activities.' We have begun to think that the virtual teaching environment could create such a possibility, whereas the conventional classroom tends to be limited in terms of incorporating real world situations. For example, Tiffin and Rajasingham (2001) envisage a virtual class embedded within a physical face-to-face class, thus allowing a group of science students in the UK to have an experience of volcanic activities in Africa via a virtual class. In this way, the praxis of the professional activities can be woven into the theory that the students may have learnt in the conventional classroom. In the process, the role of the teacher may change from that of knowledge-giver to that of a fellow knowledge-seeker and facilitator.

For example, Ashworth has experimented with public service translations both in conventional translation courses and in his most recent experimental course in Web localization at the University of Hawaii. In the latter case, students translated the Web site of the Hawaii English Language Program into Japanese and French as a public service as well as a learning experience. In this case, everyone participated in the experience, including the instructor, so that 'it was a learning experience all-around.'

We have found these approaches increasingly relevant in dealing with changes that seem to characterize the time in which we live, and the emerging teaching environment on the Internet seems to facilitate them.

VOIP as a platform for teleinterpretation

As we have discussed earlier, the current generation of VOIP technology is generally not suitable for teleinterpretation to take place. However, we could clearly see the potential once the telecommunications bandwidth issue has been resolved and there have been appropriate software developments. As we discussed in Chapter 7, the rationale for the inception of VOIP as a cheap and a lesser-quality alternative to circuit-switched telecommunications does not fit in the environment that any form of interpreting demands.

Although the state of technology was such that we were not able to carry out actual teleinterpretation, the GVU project provided us with thought-experiment opportunities to consider the University as a potential client for language facilitation and to think how it can provide the necessary service. The following section shows our needs analysis and possible solutions for globalizing the GVU.

Teleinterpretation for the GVU as the Client

The GVU envisages being able to offer courses in multilingual environments. Its courses have both asynchronous and synchronous components, and we consider the latter requirements as mainly relevant to teleintepretation.

Administration and student support

The GVU site will provide administrative and student support functionality to assist with the enrollment process, general enquiries, fee information, etc. These needs will be responded to by e-mail as well as by freephone or using a VOIP application. A different freephone and VOIP number may be allocated to each language group, with an appropriate link to a teleinterpreter. It may be necessary to indicate hours within which teleinterpreters can be accessed, unless a networked group of teleinterpreters offers 24-hour support.

In-course language support

Major requirements for the GVU will be interpretation needed for real-time lectures and seminars. This will involve not only voice-based interpretation of lectures, but also transterpreting for chat text as well as any interactive message that may be used during a lecture on the whiteboard. Given the constraint to complete the lecture within the allocated time slot, simultaneous interpreting will be preferable. The current VOIP technology works best with the participants wearing a headset and speaking through a microphone. With the courses facilitated by the teleinterpreter, the voice feed for students will need to be configured so that it is connected to the interpreter output, rather than to the lecturer output. Given that not all students in a given course will need interpretation, the best arrangement may be to create a separate voice channel that can be accessed by students who require interpretation, in a similar way to today's conference interpreting.

Issues

Some courses may require more than one language combination for interpreting. In the most desirable case, interpreting will be restricted to two languages, with the expectation that students will be fluent in at least one of these. In some cases, however, a particular student may require language assistance outside of the interpretation being provided by the GVU, and will have to rely on special language assistance. The management of teleinterpretation services is a very new concept and requires considerably more attention than we are able to devote to it at this time. Teleinterpretation is in its infancy at the moment, for the limiting reasons given above and earlier (see Chapter 7) in terms of bandwidth and other support for synchronous voice communication. These latter are problems in their own right, and once resolved, need to be integrated into the management problem referred to here.

Whether or not teleinterpretation needs to be organized at source with the GVU or with each student, the provider of teleinterpretation needs to be able to fit into the technical configuration with the VOIP system that the GVU may be using. This suggests that providing teleinterpretation will become as much a technical task involving system configuration as with the difficulties in the actual interpretation process. This could be thought of as teleinterpretation competence and teleinterpreter competence, both of which are needed to deliver the required service.

Providing teleinterpretation support for online instruction implies the possibility of designing contents along the lines of internationalization that are used in Web localization. That is, the GVU could make its course content teleinterpretation-friendly. In a sense, this is similar to using a variety of international English (or, some other internationalized language) in conventional face-to-face instructional communication. However, it would also resemble internationalization in the sense that the source language used by the teleinterpreter would be this variety of internationalized English.

Lecturers whose courses are interpreter-assisted would learn to modify their lecture structure and/or its delivery to facilitate interpretation. In face-to-face interpretation, the Sender may do this to some extent, but in an online environment, this will be manifested in a different way. For example, whiteboard communication, links to other Web sites, and the use of online text chat simultaneous with synchronous voice interpretation, can be done at a pace to allow for interpreter input.

Another possible need for teleinterpretation with the GVU is related to its approach with globalization and localization. For example, its e-commerce course could be a globalized one with English instruction for which non-English speaking students may need to use teleinterpretation as required. However, the GVU is also considering providing localized e-commerce courses in different languages. For example, its Chinese e-commerce course has been piloted. A Chinese-speaking lecturer provides this course with Chinese-speaking students in mind. It may be possible that non Chinese-speaking students could subscribe to the course with the aid of tele-interpretation. In either case, the need for teleinterpretation is specific to each student's needs, but the course itself will do well to accommodate this possibility at the onset of its design process for the synchronous components involving Translation-Mediated Communication (TMC). The final section makes a brief comment on interpreter training on the Internet.

A Virtual Course for Interpreters

This chapter has considered the virtual teaching environment on the Internet, but mainly for translators. Such courses specialized on interpretation are yet to emerge. The absence of an interpreter-oriented online course is clearly related to the difficulty in practicing interpreting in the current Internet environment. However, with the maturing of teleinterpretation platforms, such courses will clearly be needed. As we have demonstrated (see Chapter 4), it is possible to carry out transterpreting on the Internet using today's technology. This exercise will provide a taste of language facilitation for synchronous communication on the Internet. During the course of the GVU pilot, we have trialed a number of VOIP applications such as Firetalk™ and Paltalk™. They provide similar functionality with slightly different designs for user interface, such as the visual display that indicates the current speaker. Figure 8.2 shows screenshots of one of these applications. It is a Paltalk session of Somali speakers. The microphone indicates the speaker, and the hand icon is used to 'raise one's hand to speak'.

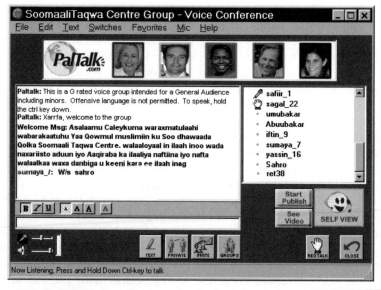

Figure 8.2 Paltalk™ showing text chat in the left window while the speaker (safiir_1) is speaking (by voice)

Since our pilot course for the GVU in 2000, a new type of voice-mail program, called PureVoice™ by QUALCOMM, has come to our attention. This technology may be of considerable value in the teaching of consecutive interpreting over the Internet. It has the feature of allowing one to insert voice recordings into an existing voice recording that can then be sent via e-mail. For example, a source of voice text in English with numbered paragraphs could be used for consecutive interpretation practice, in which the student listens to a paragraph and takes notes, and then immediately records an interpretation following that paragraph and e-mails it to the instructor.

We are hoping to be able to pursue the possibility of creating a useful practice for teleinterpreters in our next pilot experiment for the GVU. In the meantime, we can say that the challenges of designing multilingual support for online instruction themselves reflect the issues of ongoing changes in telecommunications and the need for adaptive multilingual support. We have to keep in mind that the philosophy of management of startup (as well as established) online companies involves the recognition of the need to become and remain innovative in the use of technologies. In information technology, 'change is the name of the game'. As a result, new tools for telecommunication emerge almost weekly. In this climate, both the teacher and the learner of teletranslation and teleinterpretation must remain in a constant adaptive mode for two reasons:

- ongoing shifts in the delivery of multilingual support;
- the pervasive need to deal with real-time problems when engaged in synchronous communication.

The second item above implies the need to design instructional content delivery with more than sufficient redundancy to compensate for transmission failures in synchronous communications, at least until the technology is fully stable. Since many of the real-time problems arise from the lack of sufficient bandwidth, this may no longer be an issue once the broadband information superhighway becomes a reality. In the next chapter, we will envisage what it might be like for the language support industry to operate in such an environment.

Topics for Further Research or Discussion

(1) How would it be possible to train teleinterpreters over the Internet if there was sufficient bandwidth to enable fast, reliable voice and video transmissions?

(2) List all of the ways in which teleinterpreters could become involved in

interpreting voice communications in a telecommunications environment that included the above voice and video transmissions, voice mail, webcasts of the news and cell phone conversations using cell phones with Web displays.

(3) Design a project that involves teletranslators situated in: Hong Kong, New Delhi, Jerusalem, Venice, Marseilles, Yokohama, Roanoake (Virginia), Honolulu and Waikato (New Zealand). This would be a newsletter for investors on international exchanges that must reach them at least two hours before their market opens every day. The newsletter would appear in Chinese, English, Japanese, Italian, French, and Spanish. The information sources for the newsletter would come from these languages, and would be compiled into a multilingual draft for translation into these languages in a timely manner. How would you set up the teletranslator community to handle this challenge? What factors would be involved?

Chapter 9

Global Information Society and the New Paradigm of Language Support

In this chapter we shift gears to a future mode to address the role of Translation as teletranslation and teleinterpretation in the information society. The information society can be defined in different ways depending on the focus, ranging from economic to technological, social, political and cultural dimensions. Here, we define the information society as one based on an infrastructure of IT where people place greater reliance on the telecommunications system than on the physical transport system (Wang & Dordick, 1993; Tiffin & Rajasingham, 1995). As such, our focus is on technological influences on the infrastructure of the society, and their linguistic and cultural consequences. The indications are that the geographical location of communicators is becoming increasingly irrelevant as they move into cyberspace, which is independent of physical location and less dependent on time. At the same time, this move exposes everyone to a great array of languages.

Europe has been addressing this issue through a number of official programs. For example, a report *Europe and the Global Information Society* (1994; available at http://www.ispo.cec.be/infosoc/backg/bangeman.html) reflects the interest in the social, cultural and linguistic aspects of the information society. The lack of (sufficient) language support is seen as undermining the capability afforded by the information infrastructure to facilitate global communications. Our assumption is that in the future information society, both multinationals and other organizations that may have sophisticated language management in place, as well as individuals whose lifestyle relies on a range of virtual interactions in cyberspace, will become increasingly subject to Translation-mediated Communication (TMC).

Our assumption is that the future society will be global in nature, based upon an extensive information infrastructure, and that there will be a great need to overcome language and cultural barriers in a variety of virtual interactions between people. This chapter provides a future vision of the paradigm of teletranslation and teleinterpretation when we move into the global information society based on the ubiquitous broadband information infrastructure.

Paradigm Shift

We have been pursuing the signs of the emergence of a new paradigm of Translation in order to construct a cohesive picture of the future of Translation. When we use the term 'new paradigm' we may be viewed as overstating the change that is taking place. The term paradigm, as used by Kuhn (1962), denotes the core set of concepts adopted by scientists as the dominant ontological model at a given historical moment. When scientists discover anomalies that do not fit into the old paradigm, it becomes necessary for them to think in terms of a new paradigm. Our use of 'paradigm shift' is based on Kuhn, as we consider that full-fledged teletranslation and teleinterpretation belong to a different paradigm from the conventional practices of Translation as they are driven by an entirely different communication infrastructure. Kuhn's concept provided a fresh interpretation of how new scientific discoveries were made, not as an evolutionary continuum, but as a revolutionary breakthrough from the previous paradigm. In this way, Kuhn suggested that scientific progress could be seen in terms of a chain of paradigm shifts within which each paradigm is mutually exclusive. In what follows, we will further qualify our use of the term 'paradigm' in this book.

The major change that has taken place in the translation industry has resulted from the emerging types of communication engendered by the Internet. As we pointed out earlier, electronic literacy defines the types of knowledge and skills that an individual needs in order to utilize the electronic, i.e. the Internet, environment. Naturally, people's communication behavior is different from their behavior in face-to-face communication, in writing and mailing letters through the post office, sending faxes, ringing the phone and leaving a message, and the like. Now that we can use mobile phones for an immediate link or e-mail to reach persons at the earliest convenient moment for them, we do not have to rely so heavily on the fixed-line telephone for communication, which so often results in 'telephone tag.' We can combine voice and text in synchronous communication with people located anywhere in the world. Therefore, in this sense, there has been a shift in our communication behaviors.

A 'paradigm shift' occurs when the parties to this kind of innovation begin to realize that the entire concept of communication has undergone a major change. We are perhaps at the beginning of such a change, perhaps it is an incipient 'paradigm shift' – it is still too early to tell. As discussed in an article on 'Internet time' in *Technology Review* (see http://www.techreview.com), the engineers and technology people can clearly, and often correctly, visualize the implications and potential impact of their innovations on their world.

But, as always, it takes time for others (the users of innovations) to see it, usually after some resistance. It is easy to understand why the technologists talk about paradigm shifts, since these have occurred in *their* understanding. A paradigm shift in language support with establishment of teletranslation and particularly teleinterpretation will have to wait at least until further developments of the infrastructure to allow multilingual and multimodal communication at a distance. Our concept of the emergence of a new paradigm of Translation in relation to the information society is illustrated in Figure 9.1.

Kuhn regards the creation of a new paradigm as a revolutionary process, but this depends on the point from which the paradigm is viewed. Once it is well established, the new paradigm appears independent of the old one. And yet, in its creation, it seems to follow an evolutionary continuum from the old paradigm. For example, we will not be able to identify precisely the day when we enter the information society as the shift will be a gradual one but, for people who only know the information society, the industrial society may seem to have nothing in common with its successor. In this sense, when we talk about the new paradigm of Translation, we are imagining the point when it is well established and has become normal practice rather than an anomaly for translators and interpreters.

Localization and its associated processes can be considered as a new paradigm that is now well established within the language industry. Although it has elements of conventional translation, it cannot be explained entirely on the basis of the conventional paradigm of translation. Software companies began to employ the localization process in the 1980s, but it was not until the late 1990s that it began to be included by some

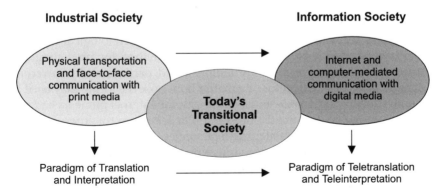

Figure. 9.1 A shift to information society and a new paradigm of teletranslation and teleinterpretation

institutions as an academic topic for translation studies (thus subject to theorization). In the meantime, the localization industry has continued to grow, and has established its own business models and best practices, largely without reliance on knowledge of conventional translation.

Rethinking the paradigmatic basis for a professional field of activities implies rethinking the theoretical basis. We have found that the field of localization provides an excellent opportunity to rethink translation theories. As we have highlighted, such concepts as language management at the user end and internationalization stemming from localization are significant developments that are pushing the boundaries of the conventional translation practice. They therefore provide an insight into future developments. Localization is driven by market forces, by capabilities afforded by IT, and by the clients who dictate what they want from language support providers. In the future, new innovations on the Internet such as voice applications, Web platforms or wireless links and developments yet to appear on the drawing board will also contribute to a new mode of language support. The direction of future developments may therefore lie in the combination of today's emergent trends and future innovations. This leads to our next topic of how to research the future.

Studying the Future

Understanding the nature of the change that is taking place all around translators and interpreters will better prepare them to face further challenges. This also applies to entrepreneurs who wish to develop language services in the Internet environment in consideration of emerging needs and applications of state-of-the-art technology. Such understanding will be important also for educators of future language professionals as the gap between what they teach and what the market expects of translators and interpreters needs to be reduced. With fast-moving technological environments, we are today in ever more need of a method for predicting the future. And yet, as has been amply demonstrated, particularly by the recent rises and falls of the 'dot-coms,' no matter how close the future may be, it is by definition unpredictable. In a similar way, the Internet pioneers had not expected e-mail to become the most popular feature of the Internet. On a smaller scale, the exponential growth of wireless Internet services in Japan belongs to the same surprise scenario, which became a reality. We need to be mindful that 'it is often the unforeseen outcomes of revolutions that make the biggest impact' (Webb & Graham-Rowe, 2000).

So, how can we build a future vision which will help prepare the language profession for the future? One research tool available is a 'futures scenario' within futures research methodology. With its application by the military and later in the civil domain by RAND Corporation (The Futures Group, 1994), scenario planning has a long history. Scenario analysis has since evolved from the 'predict-and-control' rationalistic process based on the most likely projection to the searching process which seeks 'enhanced understanding of the changing structures in society' where scenario planning relies on qualitative causal thinking rather than on probability (Van der Heijden, 1996). The scenario can be regarded as a 'perception device' that allows plausible pictures to emerge based on causal thinking that reflects different interpretations of key phenomena (Van der Heijden, 1996). The increasing popularity of scenario-based thinking seems to lie in the fact that it recognizes the uncertainty and complexity involved in analyzing the future, as compared with forecasting methods which tend to 'box in' uncertainties and assume that there is one right answer (Van der Heijden, 1996). A scenario is a narrative description of the future in which the observer is allowed to visualize a given system at some fixed point in the future and, by extrapolating from the trends in the past, to show it is a viable possibility for the future (Tiffin & Rajasingham, 1995).

Another dimension of scenarios is that they are used to challenge the mental models one may have about the future (Schwartz, 1996). Similarly, scenarios help to overcome 'embedded perceptual limitations' by introducing a new perspective, and add new 'memories of the future' (Van der Heijden, 1996). As we have observed, many language service providers today operate in conventional mode and also offer teletranslation, catering to the emergent needs arising from the Internet. They may be trying out new tools such as Translation Memory and working with partners who can provide internationalization services. Out of these experiences will arise a new practice that caters to the new needs, and better practice will result. Since our aim in this book was to further stimulate the readers' thinking about the future, we are providing a hypothetical future with scenarios. The following is our attempt at explaining one possible course of future for translators and interpreters.

Future Scenarios

Given that a scenario-based approach is better suited to analyze a midterm to longer-term future than a short-term one, where 'a level of predictability and a significant uncertainty coexist' (Van der Heijden, 1996), we will set a period of time for our scenarios around 2010 to 2015. By then, the Internet is expected to have become broadband with the progressive development of Internet II.

The Internet has been developing continuously since the mid-1990s, but we are today (mid-2001) still awaiting a full-fledged information society supported by a much more sophisticated information infrastructure. This should allow vast amounts of information to travel rapidly in a chosen form, be it text, speech or image whenever and wherever the Sender wishes to transmit the Message. Today, in reality, our e-mail fails when we least expect it, and voice applications on the Internet are, as we have explained, only hit and miss. In envisaging teletranslation and teleinterpretation, our assumption is that their dominant operating environment will be characterized by digital communications networks that are much more advanced than today's Internet, with increasingly fast and powerful computers supported via advanced telecommunications networks. We will first outline what we consider to be major factors involved in the shift from the old to the new paradigm. In particular, in order to incorporate the perspectives of both the provider and the user of language support, we consider the change in terms of process requirements and service requirements as depicted in Table 9.1. The former reflects the processing capabilities of the providers, and the latter refers to service/product expectations of the users.

From the provider's perspective, literacy on the part of translators and interpreters in at least two languages had been a basic requirement, meaning that they could read and write with the print-based media. But increasingly translators needed to become computer literate, and now it is becoming increasingly necessary for them to be literate with digital media so that they are able to process various digital content that is subject to language facilitation. In Chapter 4, we discussed the possible development of an online sublanguage common in CMC modes such as e-mail and chat. Similarly, Snell-Hornby (2000: 12) observes the influence of the Internet on English language as the development of 'McLanguage' or 'McEnglish' which is 'reduced in stylistic range and subject matter, and – with the aid of abbreviations, icons, acronyms and graphic design – tailor-made for fast consumption.' The Translator who serves these communication modes may also be required to understand the Message written in McEnglish as the source text and sometimes may also be required to create the Message in it as the target text.

Computers have increasingly assisted the work of translators. Computer-assisted translation will extend into the translators' workspace only with further integration of various tools to optimize the human inputs and machine aid. Furthermore, such tools will increasingly become networked, as is already happening with Translation Memory. This will partly stem from distributed workforces and the sharing of centralized databases and various management systems.

Table. 9.1 The shift to the new paradigm of language support

Today's paradigm	New paradigm
Process requirements	
Print media literacy	Digital media literacy
Computer-assisted	Network-assisted
Some engineering inputs	Extensive engineering inputs
Implicit culturalization	Explicit culturalization
Text- or speech-based	Mixed mode with text and speech
Service requirements	
Single-level facilitation	Multi-level facilitation
Downstream service	Upstream service
Value-added unclear	High value-added
Word-based billing	Sales-based billing
One-to-one delivery	One-to-many distribution
Increasing English literacy	Prevalent English literacy

In terms of producing the end product, engineering processes are increasingly required, as in the case of localization of digital media. Another development that comes from the digital content is the need for culturalization of the content, in particular that of non-textual elements. The previously-implicit manipulation of non-textual elements in translation will become much more explicit as digital technology allows sophisticated manipulations. Web localization is already addressing this issue with non-textual elements such as icons, graphics or the overall design of the site. High value-added language support will be one that combines engineering and culturalization to achieve TMC in the most efficient and effective manner.

The last point is that, in real-time interactions involving voice and text chat, language support will be sought in synchronous speech and text modes. This will demand a combined service of translation and interpretation, blurring the current boundary of the two. Furthermore, the hybrid mode of transterpreting may sometimes be needed. These will all constitute new skills and knowledge for the part of translators and interpreters.

The user's perspective may be summarized in terms of service and end-product requirements. As part of language management, multi-level language facilitation has emerged, as in the case of differing levels of software localization being implemented according to the size of the target market. Similarly, language support in general will need to be able to cater to varying needs with a multi-level service depending on the purpose of the given TMC as determined by the client. It may range from MT-based gisting to highly sophisticated globalization services. Multi-level facilitation also means personalization of the service to cater to different needs of the users. Today, a degree of personalization is achieved with the use of various agents that are realized in computer software. Many e-commerce sites are already using the technology to analyze and store a particular customer's shopping pattern or taste in products, while search engines may use agents to find information specified by a particular user. A new development taking place on the Web called 'Semantic Web,' which augments the current 'human user'-oriented Web data to become intelligible to computers (Berners-Lee *et al.*, 2001) is also expected to allow the increased use of such agents.

It seems likely that major users of language support will continue to upstream language facilitation in order to keep their spending on localization and translation under control, and their application more efficient and effective. The users may employ off-the-shelf products to implement a global management infrastructure (see the ASP model in Chapter 6) into which language support providers will be expected to fit. The upstreaming trend may also occur at an individual user level with the use of MT and MI (Machine Interpretation), for example. This may happen in the sense that the users will learn the characteristics of each computer tool and adjust their Messages to be more machine-friendly by editing them or altering their speech. This may also mean the use of interactive authoring systems. For example, the Universal Networking Language (UNL)[1] being developed by United Nations University in Tokyo in collaboration with several research institutions of the world has a feature to eliminate at the authoring stage various aspects that are not translation-friendly (Joscelyne, 1999).

Another trend is for customers to seek a higher value-added language service. The value may be judged in terms of seamless engineering work combined with translation, as in the case of software or Web localization. With conventional language support, print-based translation did not involve any engineering task, and the translation was generally treated as separate from globalization. With teletranslation, the content subject to translation itself needs to be usable in a given linguistic digital environment, thus requiring engineering and linguistic adjustments. Thus, globalization service providers will tend to be perceived as offering more value-added services than the conventional language support, which would not provide such engineering work (see POTS in Chapter 6). While plug-in applications as in the case of the ASP model appear to be providing the infrastructure for language management for organizations (see Chapter 6), even the automated solutions require users to know the specific role of TMC that is unique to their organizations.

This intimate link developing between language facilitation and organizations' products may result in a different charging basis. Currently by far the most common way to charge for translation is based on wordage. This may change, at least for asynchronous language support, to a royalty-based system that links the language support much more directly to the sales – as suggested by some localizers (LISA, 2000). This kind of change has taken place with telecommunications whereby time-based charging is replaced by data-based charging.

Another new direction may be that one-to-one language support will become a one-to-many distributed service. Such examples already exist in the case of MT-based services accompanying various search engines on the Internet. Another example may stem from the extensive use of Translation Memory or a large-scale parallel text corpus that may be utilized directly by translation users. This will in effect create the situation in which a translation provided by one translator (with the results stored in a shareable TM system) caters to many users. The translation service providers currently use TM systems, but in future the users of translation services may directly access translation via TM. This comes close to the concept of example-based MT (EBMT).

Another factor is the continuing trend of English to be the lingua franca of the world. Given that the fundamental need for Translation comes from the lack of common language between the Sender and the Receiver of the Message, we cannot escape the debate over the spread of English as a global language (Crystal, 1997; Schäffner, 2000). With the accompanying increase in the number of people learning English, it is likely that more people will be using English in future as a means of communication, albeit at varying levels of competency. The popularity of English is already producing 'international English' which functions 'as a basic common denominator for supra-cultural communication' (Schäffner, 2000)[2].

Similarly, Dertouzos (1997: 283) suggests that the virtual communication space in cyberspace (which he calls the Information Marketplace) will 'superimpose a cultural veneer of shared experiences on top of the individual cultures of the world' as English has become 'a common bond for the member nations of the European Union which all retain their own languages and customs.' In other words, people may use English as a utility for interacting in cyberspace with those who do not share the same language and culture. However, when these same people go back to their physical world, they will adhere to their mother tongues. It seems likely then that the prevalent use of English by the world's population will eliminate the need for Translation in certain sectors of today's Translation market.

The prevalence of English is likely to manifest itself in more cases where the Sender creates the Message in English, which is not his or her first language (this is sometimes called L2 authoring). This is a known practice observed in some international organizations such as the United Nations or the European Commission.[3] The Sender needs to be aware that L2 authoring may introduce a new type of 'noise' in Translation. L2 authoring to create the Message in English may also be used in order to eliminate the need for Translation where the Receiver is again not a native English speaker. It can further introduce problems with intelligent agents if the latter are not programmed to recognize varieties of International English.

Based on the factors discussed above and in earlier chapters, the following narratives provide scenarios of teletranslation and teleinterpretation at work.

Scenario 1: In-house teletranslator

Mariko is an in-house teletranslator based in Sydney working for a multinational globalization solution company whose headquarters are in Amsterdam. She is Japanese and her working languages include English and Chinese. Her company set her up with a high-end laptop with both land-based and mobile access to the Internet and the company's Intranet. She has just finished an intensive diploma course on one aspect of Eastern medical science. She has a degree in chemistry but her work was increasingly in the wider area of medical science, particularly based on Chinese medicine, requiring her to have more specific subject knowledge. This course was offered by the Hong Kong Virtual University, and allowed her to do the entire course remotely. In addition to assignments, which were primarily delivered by e-mail, she had to attend twice-weekly synchronous virtual seminars linking all students to the lecturer via a desktop conferencing system. She chose the English track, but the course was also offered in Chinese and Japanese. The Japanese track was conducted with synchronous interpretation service.

This is not Mariko's first experience in taking virtual courses. It has become important for translators to continue with ongoing professional development efforts as their work is becoming increasingly specialized and also the competition is getting stiff against translators based all over the world.

Her routine as a teletranslator involves becoming familiar with her client's globalization process and a language and content management system. Her clients are mostly large pharmaceutical companies that tend to have proprietary content management systems according to which her translation inputs and outputs are configured to fit. In particular, she needs to learn the company-specific control language to allow her own translation outputs to be MT-friendly. This is to anticipate the use of MT by some recipients of the translation. Mariko has been trained in the use of Translation Memory systems, which have become far easier to use compared with earlier generation of TM. She mainly translates online documents for product information and also facilitates a weekly user forum on chat as a transterpreter for one pharmaceutical firm. Her work also involves a great deal of collaboration with her colleagues in virtual environments. She shares computer files and databases with them, and her work progress is monitored by the centralized document globalization system. Generally teletranslators are expected to be literate with a wide range of digital environments. In fact, the profession now includes an increasing number of people who are proficient with some computer languages.

Scenario 2: Translation engineer

Richard is American and is based in Bangkok working as a translation engineer. He receives his work mainly through word of mouth, albeit virtual, and through his multimedia site on the Internet. He has a degree in computational linguistics and a graduate translation diploma. His working languages are Chinese and French. He is also armed with a good understanding of Thai culture. His work requires a good grasp of the clients' TMC needs through their globalization strategies and localization targets. Richard designs organization-specific language management systems as well as the customization of various machine translation systems the organization wishes to use. His clients are mainly medium-to-large organizations, but also include freelance teletranslators and teleinterpreters who need to have their tools customized. For example, he recently worked for a teleinterpreter who needed to have her WAP device linked to the interpretation memory stored in her PC.

To keep up with rapid changes in the computing and telecommunications technology, Richard often takes short courses using virtual flexible learning systems. Unlike computational linguists a generation before him, Richard is also familiar with culturalization of multimedia products. Being a former PlayStation aficionado and a computer-game expert, he has acquired understanding of culture-specific features with graphics and virtual environments. These jobs require inputs in non-textual visual aesthetics in his specialized languages and cultures targeting the USA, Chinese or French-speaking markets.

Scenario 3: Freelance teletransterpreter

Lynn is an American Japanese based in Honolulu. She works as an interpreter for English and Japanese on the Internet facilitating international virtual meetings and also occasionally works in face-to-face conferences performing simultaneous interpreting. She has a young family and her work mode as a remote language facilitator suits her better than being a physical presence-based interpreter having to travel. She is registered with a number of teleinterpretation companies whose main shop fronts are virtual sites on the Internet. Since the Internet has improved considerably to support multimodal broadband communications, an increasing number of international conferences and meetings have adopted a virtual mode for certain types of gatherings.

Lynn used to work as a court interpreter and is specialized in legal interpretation although she now accepts other kinds of work. One clear trend now is that more people are able to speak English and her role therefore is often as facilitator in meetings where fine legal points may need clarification. For example, many young Japanese lawyers trained for international arbitration speak good enough English, but they sometimes prefer to have Lynn sitting along side them (albeit virtually) just in case. Other meetings she assists include annual general meetings for shareholders for multinationals, which involve a mixture of presentation using static text and synchronous text-chat in addition to voice presentations. In these meetings, off-site shareholders who are participating virtually are able to ask questions in their respective languages in both text and voice mode, which Lynn interprets in an appropriate mode. For these meetings to cover a large number of off-site participants, a large pool of transterpreters working from different locations is engaged. It took her a dozen training sessions to get used to multitasking, switching from text to speech or doing synchronous text transterpreting. Transterpreters like Lynn are required to be familiar with multimodal platforms used on the Internet, and teleinterpretation companies often provide specialized training.

The above scenarios are intended to provide snapshots of language-support professionals working in teletranslation and teleintepretation in the next decade. The role of language facilitation, as we call teletranslation and teleinterpretation in a global information society, is to serve seamlessly in the digital environment for a variety of CMC. The new dimension emerging from this role of the teletranslator or teleinterpreter may be summarized as:

(1)   a high level of digital literacy, in particular, familiarity with given communication modes;
(2)   an understanding of the context of the Message and the client's TMC needs;
(3)   an understanding of wider cultural issues which concern packaging of the given Message; and
(4)   an increasing need for subject matter specialization and commitment to ongoing professional development.

When we look at the role of language support in the information society, the most notable change may be in terms of ubiquity of TMC, as it becomes an integral part of people's communication activities, many of which may take place in cyberspace. E-commerce companies will have localized and culturalized their virtual shop fronts. These jobs may be done by the teletranslators, as we envisaged in our first scenario. A pharmaceutical virtual site linked to telemedicine may offer detailed information on medication and related information, including the latest research. This type of job will require a subject-specialist translator who also needs to keep up with the latest developments to be able to cope with constantly updated information on the site. The translators also need to be proficient in using increasingly wide-ranging translation resources to maintain a high standard of work. Also the fact that most translation outputs may be retained in some kind of TM system will mean that any mistake made in the first place may be repeated elsewhere. In particular, in the case of the translations used for example-based MT, unsuspecting monolingual users may be provided with wrong translations. In this sense, quality control becomes even more important.

Also when e-commerce sites start to provide language support for synchronous communication modes such as voice and text chat sessions, teleinterpretation support including transterpreting will be needed. In the third scenario, a teleinterpreter was envisaged. Interpreters may find it hard to imagine working in this mode today, but if they try any of the currently available chat rooms, particularly using text and voice, they will get a taste of what may be in store. Multitasking switching between voice and text does happen in interpreting for face-to-face meetings today, but doing this in cyberspace via one's computer is different. This becomes a training issue, as does digital literacy with understanding the use of the given digital medium. As we suggested before, in some cases, the transterpreter may need to take on the role of managing the given interactions.

Our second scenario described a new professional called the translation engineer, which we mentioned in Chapter 3. Today's localization engineers provide indispensable engineering inputs to localization projects, but at the same time their lack of understanding of languages and translation issues more often than not causes problems. The industry will need professionals who understand both the engineering and translation requirements of increasingly complex localization and culturalization work.

We have tried to convey some characteristics of the changes that are possible, given the current trends and emergent developments. What we hoped to achieve with our scenarios was to give readers 'some of the flavor and details of events that might occur, without seeming too concrete about outcomes' as Hiltz and Turoff (1993)[4] explained in their use of scenarios in envisaging the implication of the then emerging Internet. In exploring the implication of the future developments of professional activities in the information society, Susskind provides a useful insight:

> ... in the short to medium term, during which we will be in the transitional phase between the print-based industrial society and the IT-based information society, the order of the day will be automation, streamlining, optimizing, and improvement of current practices. In the longer term, after this transitional phase, there will be a fundamental shift in paradigm... Then, innovation will dominate and new working practices will emerge. (Susskind, 1996: 267)

Susskind's interpretation seems applicable to Translation, which is currently undergoing a transitional phase while the language industry as a whole is striving to optimize computer and human functions to efficiently produce end products that are appropriate to the purpose of the user. In the next chapter, we will attempt to explore 'innovation and new working practices' by looking further into the future beyond the next decade of our scenarios.

Topics for Further Research or Discussion

(1) In the theory of translation, machine translation plays a minor role, as translators themselves have little regard for the efforts of linguists and engineers to produce translations that come anywhere near the

quality of the translators' human efforts. In the case of localization, which is primarily a human effort aided by translation tools, knowledge of language differences plays a major role in creating acceptable localized output. What linguistic knowledge would be valuable for the new translator-localizer in this regard? Can linguistics now play a greater role in translation theory itself?

(2) Imagine a future scenario in which Chinese language comes to play a major role in global markets. Imagine further that it will become a major language in the sense that International English is now. How could this reshape the notions of localization, internationalization, and controlled language?

(3) International English is actually a large set of varieties of English, usually in the context of English as a second language. What impact will these varieties have on language technology such as machine translation and interpretation (i.e. how will these technologies have to be modified)?

Notes

1. The UNL is a conceptual language that allows automatic translation so that academics can readily share documents and messages across different languages on the Internet.
2. It is interesting to note the widespread use of English in voice chat program sites such as Paltalk™, where Middle Eastern languages (Farsi, Arabic, Kurdish and Turkish) predominate. Even while someone is speaking, others are chatting away in text mode in a mixture of English and these languages. Given this kind of practice, one wonders what the real role of English is in international communication.
3. Such English is sometimes referred to as 'Eurolect or Eurojargon' belonging to 'European English' (Schäffner, 2000).
4. *The Network Nation* was first published in 1978.

Chapter 10
New Paradigm of Translation and Interpretation

This chapter draws together our argument that Translation (translation and interpretation) is faced with fundamental changes that spring from the emerging new infrastructure of communication. Whatever state of affairs we may present here is based merely on the configuration of communication tools on the Internet that are currently available or are most likely to appear in the near future. Discussions of developments beyond the present horizon, of course, depend on the realization of its future potentials.[1] In this chapter we discuss the possible nature of the transformation towards the new paradigm of teletranslation and teleinterpretation based on a futuristic telecommunications environment.

Elements of Change

We have explored how Translation is evolving towards teletranslation and teleinterpretation. TMC allows us to analyze the role played by Translation in terms of the Sender, the Receiver and the Message. In this section, we highlight the nature of the change that is taking place in the Message as our communicating environments become largely based on CMC. In particular, we describe the changes in terms of Gile's (1995) notion of the Message consisting of the Content and the Package (see Chapter 1).

Change in the Content of the Message: Convergence of speech and written text

The development of online chat via interactive text has presented a potential new mode of Translation, which we have called transterpreting (see Chapter 4). We have suggested that teleinterpretation is likely to include this kind of interactive text processing, which is a hybrid between translation and interpretation. Transterpreting can be seen as related to the existing mode called sight translation. Sight translation, which is sometimes performed by interpreters in face-to-face meetings, normally consists of reading a source-language text aloud in the target language (thus interpreting the written text in real-time) or consecutively interpreting a speech that has been read from a text. Similar practice can also be traced to translation produced via dictation, where the translator fluently speaks the translation to a typist or tape recorder. Today the emergence of speech-recognition technology is further facilitating this process, with the translator speaking his or her translation to the computer. In this way, this mode of producing translation orally may become more widespread.

Although computer-mediated chat as a mode of communication has only recently come into common use, the beginnings of interactive text can be seen in the use of word processors in translation production. The word processor has allowed the translation process to adopt a mode similar to oral translation, whereby the translator is able to input text spontaneously even if it is not yet well formulated. In other words, word processing allows for relatively instantaneous production of drafts that are much more easily edited than was possible on the typewriter. This gives the translator much more room to work creatively. The main difference between this situation and transterpreting is that the former has the source text available at all times whereas the chat text keeps moving as it is continuously produced in real-time. Also, the transterpreter has very little time to look up words or to go back and forth between the source and the target text. This, in fact, is a characteristic of interpretation, and so chat text as the Message tends to call for a kind of synchronous rendering more familiar to the process of interpretation than of translation. Nevertheless, both inputs and outputs are written text rather than speech, which the interpreter would normally process.

The convergence of translation and interpretation reflects in a way the incremental impact of technology on written words, as discussed in detail by Heim (1987) and Ong (1982). Halliday (1989: 81) also discusses the impact of modern technology in blurring the distinction between speech and writing. The invention of tape recorders turned speech into something more permanent and less ephemeral whereas, for the writer, seeing lines of text appear on a computer screen as they are being produced, may make previously static written text feel more like a dynamic process. While the distinction between writing and speech was originally driven by the application of technology to writing only (for example, writing implements), technology is now changing the nature of both (Halliday, 1989). For example, in order to reduce errors, the user of a speech-recognition system may develop a certain articulate way of speaking to the system. In other words, while users are expected to train the system to become accustomed to their inputs, they also learn to speak in a machine-friendly manner.

How the Message had to change to fit the medium was also illustrated in a tangible way by the recent migration of Web sites to the small screen of mobile phones; a typical Web page designed to fit a full PC screen is not suitable for viewing on the tiny screen of a mobile phone. Another unique feature seems to be the increased use of icons in Web pages adapted for viewing on the mobile screen, including in text messaging in that environment. This saves space in conveying the same amount of information as written text, as a proportion of the Content of the Message is expressed graphically (see Chapter 5). Translators who work on Web sites or on text messages for mobile phones therefore need to take such factors into consideration.

In this way, the impact of technology will continue to influence the Message that is to be translated.

Change in the Package of the Message: Articulated nonverbal context

In one sense, multimedia developments on the Internet have not progressed as fast as some people may have expected. For example, over the last few years the Internet and Web-based platforms have developed largely as text-based media, while the interactive speech mode on the Internet is still at a maturing stage. However, commercial Web pages tend to contain an increasing proportion of non-textual elements such as graphics and other types of images, as well as sounds. Multimedia Web site design involves more facets than those required for two-dimensional text-based desktop publishing because of the digital environment in which it is embedded. Multimedia content creation and design on the Web require specific technical and artistic skills, and have given rise to specialists in Web site design and development. Messages on the Web thus include a site's nonverbal design elements as well as verbalized information.

This in turn has meant that Web-site translation needs to take such nonverbal aspects into account, which makes the Package-processing task of TMC much more explicit than in paper-based two-dimensional text. A Web site that presents information in terms of text, visual images and sounds requires Translation to embrace all elements to make the Message as a whole compatible to the Receiver. Furthermore, the advancement towards broadband telecommunications with multimodal communications capabilities suggests an increasingly important role for the nonverbal components in the Message. We see this as an articulated context embedded in the nonverbal component of the Message.

Anthropologist Malinowski's (1967) concept of 'context of situation' was based on the conflicting needs that he experienced when he had to render in English the texts he collected in Kiriwinian, a language spoken in the Trobriand Islands. His free translation did not convey anything of the language or the culture, whereas the literal translation was not intelligible to English speakers. This led him to coin the term 'context of situation' to mean the entire environment of either a spoken or written message. With multimedia development, technology is now beginning to provide a way of including the context of situation. For example, a Web site can use music to provide the reader with a desired ambience, while the background wall-paper, color scheme, fonts and layout of the page are all designed to create an appropriate context of situation for the intended message.

Let us consider, for example, a problem recently encountered by one of the authors, reported by his friend. The friend had attended a ballet with a fellow student from India. After the performance, the Indian enthusiastically remarked about one of the dancers: 'she is as graceful as an elephant.' The friend could see by the tone of her voice that she was not being sarcastic, yet had some difficulty visualizing elephants as 'graceful' since in the US typically this statement would imply sarcasm. Multimedia comes to the rescue. To communicate visually the Indian girl's idea of the graceful elephant in multimedia format, all one would need is a video clip of elephants moving gracefully to reinforce the description for the non-Indian Receiver. This is a case of articulating contextual information, which the conventional Translation has normally been unable to do.

Given that the nature of the Message seems to be significantly influenced by certain characteristics of technology, we shall look beyond the next decade in search of technological developments that can further drastically influence the Content and the Package of the Message. This gives us a relevant context in which we can explore the nature of change to come with the teletranslation and teleinterpretation paradigm.

Two-Dimensional to Three-Dimensional Virtual World

We have described so far the transition from the conventional to a new paradigm of Translation. Teletranslation is already maturing on today's Internet, while teleinterpretation is still waiting in the wings as interpretation has been a 'presence-based' practice. While telephone interpreting could function effectively in certain communicative situations and circumstances such as emergency situations, it has not become a mainstream mode of interpreting, despite the ubiquity of telephones themselves. This is simply because today's telecommunications is not yet able to accommodate the proxemics equivalent to face-to-face communication. The two-dimensional cyberspace (including telephones) is still no substitute for certain presence-based interactions or activities that are strongly grounded in face-to-face interactions. We have discussed the role played by non-verbal communication in the conventional interpretation practice (see

Chapter 7), and suggested that certain communicative situations allow interpretation to take place effectively without full nonverbal cues. The paradigm of teleinterpretation as conceived so far has been based on communications technology, which is still deficient in terms of facilitating a full range of nonverbal communication.

The very technology to address this 'last mile' problem in today's tele-communication is distributed virtual reality, which allows multimodal communication at a distance. Today this technology largely belongs to laboratories, but beyond the next decade it is likely to come on to the general scene, permitting communications based on tele-presence. For example, telemedicine, which requires multimodal communication, has had extensive experimentation (see Kalawsky, 1993; Dertouzos, 1997; *The Economist*, 2001b).

In Chapter 4, we observed the precursor to this direction of technology developments in the use of avatars in chat environments such as ActiveWorlds™. These avatars provide a limited range of controllable nonverbal communication cues and of context of situations as different background scenery. The animated avatars placed in different backdrops are the next step up from emoticons, which people use today to facilitate their CMC messages in order to add more contexts for the interaction. To purists, avatars may look like a gimmick, but despite their primitiveness, their visual means of representing one's presence is proven to play a signifi-cant role in communicating at a distance, by facilitating turn-taking cues, for example (Bowers *et al.*, 1996). When it becomes possible for each communicator to be presented in a 3D image of his or her own choice and to be able to interact in a given virtual environment with certain tactile senses, the meaning of telecommunication as communication at a distance will fundamentally change. The following outlines one such technology that is being developed.

HyperReality

Research and development of distributed virtual reality has been under-taken by many major laboratories of the world, including MIT Media Lab and such projects as the National Tele-Immersion Initiative (NTII), which is led by Jaron Lanier, the virtual reality guru. In this section, we will outline one example called HyperReality (HR).

HR is a concept originally developed by Terashima (1995a, 1995b) at the Advanced Telecommunications Research Institute International (ATR) in Kansai Science City in Japan. Since then HR has been further experimented with in the Internet environment for virtual classes and conceptualized as a next-generation infrastructural technology (see Tiffin & Terashima, 2001).

From 1986 to 1996, Terashima led the Virtual Space Teleconferencing System project at ATR Communications Systems Laboratories, which produced a prototype HR system. The project was motivated by the absence in a standard videoconferencing system of certain nonverbal communication cues such as eye contact and by its limited ability to facilitate interactive tasks. The new system was designed to allow conference participants in different locations to mutually manipulate virtual objects and to retain eye contact while interacting with one another.

Behind ATR's approach is the salient feature of Japanese communication in which face-to-face interactions and so-called 'skinship' (a Japanese term used to mean communication via bodily contact of a non-sexual nature, such as between a mother and a child) is considered to have paramount importance. Today's telecommunication is therefore regarded as subordinate to physical face-to-face communication. ATR's overall goal is to turn telecommunication into a superior medium of communication. This background is embedded in the philosophy behind the conceptualization of HyperReality, with its emphasis on conveying nonverbal communication elements at a distance.

In HR environments, a life-size virtual image of each participant is projected on a large screen placed in each location. The images appear realistic because they are reproduced from a database in which relevant images of people and objects are stored in advance and recreated using computer graphics. The pre-stored information is asynchronously downloaded to each participant's site while real-time information, such as facial and body movements, is superimposed synchronously on the stored images and transmitted in real-time. The participants wear shutter glasses to obtain 3D images, head-tracking gear and facial-tracking sensors to send real-time information on movements from these body parts. Since 1997, HR has been used on an experimental basis via the Internet between New Zealand and Japan as a technology to support a virtual class that requires real-time interactions. Avatars of teachers and students can manipulate certain virtual objects at a distance and are able to engage in discussions using both speech and text. The NTII project is trying to achieve similar results, in particular in the environment of the Internet II, which is being developed in the USA as the next-generation Internet providing broadband transmission capabilities (Ananthaswamy, 2000).

The relevance of distributed virtual reality to Translation is that it aims to allow face-to-face interactions to operate in CMC at a distance. This will provide a suitable environment in which presence-based tasks such as interpreting can be considered. In this way, distributed virtual reality provides a specific new dimension, which is relevant to our discussion.

Translation in distributed virtual reality

Given that the technology does not as yet exist, the following discussion is limited to some extent to thought experiments. It focuses on two particular aspects of generic features of distributed virtual reality: augmentable settings, and multisensory virtual environments.

Augmentable settings

When we enter a chat room such as ActiveWorlds or Comic Chat (see Figure 4.1) with our own avatars representing our presence in a virtual world, we realize that our nonverbal communication cues suddenly become subject to more conscious decisions than probably is true in face-to-face interactions. This is simply because in virtual worlds nonverbal cues are something artificially controlled as compared with spontaneous reactions in physical environments (i.e. the participant becomes more aware of the choices to make on the nonverbal plane). Furthermore, the ability to create virtual objects and settings in virtual environments means that certain details need to be determined. These may include anything from setting out a meeting room (the positions of chairs and desks) to choosing the color of the room's wallpaper. In other words, certain arbitrary elements in physical reality become more deliberate in virtual environments because they need to be built up pixel by pixel. At the same time, such capabilities may provide the means for the Translator to entirely localize the Package element of the Message. For example, the Translator may be able to suggest a design of a meeting room to allow for optimal TMC in terms of certain cultural perspectives of the participants of the meeting.

Media translation such as subtitling or dubbing for audiovisual media currently does not allow the Translator to change the visual image on the screen, even though the image may not make sense to a Receiver who does not share the same cultural background as the Sender. While the Translator's task is to produce subtitles to establish coherence between image and words, the image remains unchanged. Similarly, interpreters are normally not able to change nonverbal cues displayed by the Sender, even though the Receiver may be baffled or even misled by them. For example, a Japanese Sender may show a big smile that contradicts the Message, which is conveying the opposite emotion. This may be due to the fact that the Japanese tend to hide negative emotions, and sometimes replace them with a smile as a mask according to unique display rules (Ekman & Friesen, 1972). Consecutive interpreting allows the Receiver to subsequently see the interpreter's nonverbal cues, which are matched with the interpreter's verbal outputs. By contrast, simultaneous interpreting will allow only the interpreter's voice, and not his or her nonverbal cues, to be heard by the Receiver, who instead is fed with the Sender's nonverbal cues.

Distributed virtual reality environments offer new possibilities. Language mediators in such environments could change the Sender's nonverbal Package in addition to rendering the verbal Content if the actual movement of the Sender appeared on the teleinterpreter's 'desktop' and the teleinterpreter could 'take it from there' and modify any undesirable nonverbal communication. The Sender might also be able to choose an avatar that is localized into the Receiver's cultural context with a set of appropriate nonverbal cues while the overall settings of the meeting are also made more familiar to the Receiver. For example, an avatar application may be programmed to either modify or filter out certain nonverbal communication depending on the Receiver's cultural context. An American executive (his avatar) who is prone to put his feet up on the table may be modified to be sitting with his legs down when talking to a group of Chinese executives. Or a teleinterpreter for a Japanese president who laughs in the wrong places (in the American context) when talking to his American counterpart may be able to replace the laughter with more appropriate facial expressions. There may also be cases where, for example, behavior on the part of one participant is undesirable/offensive to participants from another culture, and the teleinterpreter knows this. The teleinterpreter who also assumes the role of moderator may take the liberty of minimizing or obliterating that behavior electronically (e.g. excessive gesturing, coming too close or going too far away from the addressee, or using gestures that have obscene or offensive connotations in the target culture).

In this way, the nature of TMC may change significantly, making it much closer to intra-lingual communication where the Sender and the Receiver share the same cultural backgrounds, and making the Package rendition components much more explicit for language facilitators than today's Content-centred practice does.

Multisensory virtual environments

Among the advanced features of distributed virtual reality will be the realization of multisensory communication such as haptic, and possibly olfactory, senses enabled at a distance. These will be part of nonverbal information in a broader sense. For example, research is under way to permit haptic sensations when manipulating virtual objects (see Kalawsky, 1993). Development of an electronic nose that uses chemical sensors and artificial neural networks is also under way (Database, 1998). Such technology is considered important for telemedicine, mine-hazard detection and quality control in the food, beverage and perfume industries.

Although an interpreter's perception of nonverbal communication relating to paralanguage and kinesics is immediately linked to the processing of speech in face-to-face interactions, the function of tactile and olfactory senses does not seem to have attracted much attention in examining the interpretation process. However, the role of such senses becomes important for certain assignments where interactions are in large part based on the understanding of touch or smell. Language facilitation for cases such as televisits to factories producing chemicals, perfumes or wine, tele-adventure or telecooking lessons may benefit from certain tactile and olfactory information. Today's telephone interpreting or VOIP platforms applied to these situations would clearly suffer from the significantly reduced contextual information. We may see these elements becoming incorporated first into new versions of multimedia.

The impact of the multisensory information will be somewhat different for translators, essentially because their work does not depend on real-time physical interactions with the communicating parties and the surroundings. One likely impact on the translator may be in the direction of multimedia and multimodal presentation of information embedded in text. For example, today's Web sites may evolve to include both sensory and olfactory information. A patent document with such information may allow the Receiver to 'experience' the invention in virtual environments, or a future bakery Web site could be furnished with olfactory and tactile sensations whereby the visitor can smell the freshly baked bread and feel its texture. This in turn will allow translators to better understand the verbal descriptions and in fact may eliminate the need for language facilitation altogether in some cases.

Such features could also be used for dictionaries and encyclopedias, and translators and interpreters in turn could learn new terminology or words in a much more holistic way than the purely cognitive way of reading a definition expressed only in words and two-dimensional illustrations. For example, a new generation lexicon may allow body-based experience of a word in an appropriate virtual environment. This may provide a short cut to developing 'gut feeling' with new words and terminology.

Possibilities in the New Paradigm

Even if the whole communications environment is transformed, the basic and unchanging role of the Translator will be to facilitate communication between the Sender and the Receiver of the Message. However, in the conventional setting in which translation and interpretation would occur, the Sender, the Translator and the Receiver would each create their own world of meaning. By allowing more sophisticated multimedia and multimodal means of communication, emerging communications environments seem to be facilitating more ways to clarify intended meaning (think of much more sophisticated ways to explain our earlier example with the 'elephant' metaphor). They have the potential to refine/define/augment the context of situation in ways not possible with 'conventional' multimedia. It is an empirical question whether such augmentation will facilitate (multilingual) TMC.

Fillmore's (1977) theory of meaning known as 'scenes-and-frames semantics' seems relevant to explain this process. He explains the process of text analysis as follows:

> What happens when one comprehends a text is that one mentally creates a kind of world; the properties of this world may depend quite a bit on the individual interpreter's own private experiences – a reality which should account for part of the same text. As one continues with the text, the details of this world get filled in, expectations get set up which are later fulfilled or thwarted or left hanging... (Fillmore, 1977: 61)

According to Fillmore, the message provides the reader with a 'frame,' defined as 'any system of linguistic choices', on which the reader activates his or her own scenes of mentally created pictures. As admitted by Fillmore, the term 'scene' is used in 'maximally general sense' encompassing not only visual scenes but ... any kind of coherent segment ... of human beliefs, actions, experiences, or imaginings.' Using this concept, Fillmore explains the process of communication as involving 'the activation, within speakers and across speakers, of linguistic frames and cognitive scenes. Communicators operate on these scenes and frames...' (Fillmore, 1977: 66).

In the context of Translation, this approach explains how the linguistic form of the message is linked to the experience and interpretation specific to the Receiver. It also acknowledges the difficulty involved in communication, either intra-lingual or inter-lingual, since there is no way to ensure that the scenes between the Sender and the Receiver of the Message are shared. Furthermore, for inter-lingual communication, the Translator ideally needs to match scenes across two different languages. The role of the Translators is doublefold in that they evoke their own scenes from the frames of the Message in the source language, and encode them into the relevant frames of the target language. This in turn should allow appropriate scenes to be evoked by the Receiver of the Message.

Vermeer (1992) applies Fillmore's theory to explain the translation process of nonverbal communication expressed in written texts and suggests that distorted scenes evoked by the translator will lead to mistranslation, while pointing out that the error can also occur in frames. Vermeer (1992: 288) asserts that the translator's failure to imagine the scene of a particular nonverbal behavior described in the source text will mean that the Receiver cannot build up his or her scene of that particular behavior. Similarly, Seleskovitch explains the role of the scene in interpretation:

> The conceptual image that the interpreter visualizes and converts into language will similarly evoke an image in the minds of those listening to him; the image he visualizes will be colored by their own experiences, but the image may well correspond to the image they would have visualized if they had heard the original words. (Seleskovitch, 1994: 49)

This is the ideal situation for TMC to achieve. It can be argued that the ultimate goal for the Translator has been to produce frames in the target language that will evoke in the Receiver scenes that match those intended by the Sender. The Translator has so far had no means other than words to accomplish this task, although for some interpreting situations the interpreter's nonverbal cues may have played a role (Viaggio, 1997a). In comparison with this situation, emerging CMC based on multimodal capabilities could allow the Translation function to acquire new means to facilitate the matching of the scenes by adding nonverbal and contextual information.

Given the heavy information-processing load that the interpreter normally has (Gile, 1995), this may mean that a second interpreter is needed to work exclusively on nonverbal conversions as a way of adjusting nonverbal cues and contextual elements. This will create a sophisticated real-time inter-lingual and inter-cultural communication facilitation whereby not only the frames (Content) but also the scenes (Package) are changed, by manipulating nonverbal cues and contextual information. However, this would be a real challenge for the coordination and management of interpretation. In other cases, the Sender and the Receiver themselves may start exploring each other's understanding of the intended meaning of the Message, taking advantage of the capabilities endowed in the shared mediated communication space that allows multimedia and multimodal communications. Such environments may encourage the communicating parties to compare the scenes of the Sender with those of the Receiver when communicators feel that they are not on the same wavelength. Early signs of this kind of process are implied by Schrage, who maintains that shared space mediated by technology promotes exploration of shared meaning:

A flexible collaborative tool – one that facilitates the easy display of both words and images – improves the chances for creating a shared understanding. More explicitly, it gives participants from different cultures a medium to search for and create shared meaning... (Schrage, 1990: 131)

In multimedia and multimodal communications environments, the need for the Translator to rely on frames or words to convey intended meaning could be reduced by articulated nonverbal cues and contextual information. This fits the explanation given by Hall (1976) for 'HC (high context) communication' where less detailed word-based frame-to-frame explanations are required, since the context of situation is shared between the communicating parties. Such capabilities will be applicable not only to affective communication but also to facts-oriented technical communication where asymmetry of technical domains is recognized to exist across languages (Melby, 1995). In this sense, new CMC environments could provide a platform for language facilitation that is superior to that in face-to-face physical environments.

The reorientation of Translation function from being strongly frame-to-fame focused towards a more scene-to-scene approach will represent a major transformation of the profession, and may become a major characteristic of the new paradigm.

Key Issues for Translation-mediated Communication

We have explored the future of Translation using the framework of TMC. As is explicit in this approach, we have stressed that technology is an inescapable future for Translation and Translator. And yet, the most difficult question surrounding the profession is the extent of automation in language processing, which is intertwined with the notion of quality. In what follows, we hope to address these two aspects, which we consider to have a long-term implication for the development of the profession.

Issue of quality

Quality of translation has been considered as not readily quantifiable in the sense that there is always more than one way to translate the same sentence. By comparison, because of its interactive nature, interpretation has had more immediate means of receiving user feedback. The emergence of the localization industry has had a significant influence through its efforts to quantify and benchmark the quality of translation (see Chapter 6). As a result, many translation operators are ISO (International Standardization Organization) accredited, or striving to gain such accreditation (see

O'Hagan, 1997). Such trends clearly point to the difference between the modern translation operation and the traditional practice, which used to be a cottage industry that relied on pen and paper and largely on the individual talents of translators. In those days, the quality was something intangible, determined by the perception of the translator. However, more customer-oriented approaches have come to mean that the quality must match the client's requirements and not the subjective judgement applied by the translator. In software localization, the failure of localization may be much more clearly displayed than in standard translation, when the given software does not function in a user's computing environment or when the user cannot make the software work because of poor translation of the manual (although this may also be due to a poorly written source text).

The meaning of quality has changed over the years. For example, when the ALPAC (Automatic Language Processing Advisory Committee) report was released in the USA in 1966, the ALPAC had not anticipated the use of poor translations such as those produced by some MT programs. In other words, the ALPAC considered less-than-perfectly-translated text as unacceptable. And yet in today's translation market it is widely recognized that there is a place for such translations, for example in the 'gisting' of information. Translation competence as producing acceptable translations, however defined (Kiraly, 2000a), therefore means something different today from the time of the ALPAC report and may change again in the future.

One emerging trend is that clients are becoming increasingly clear about what they want translation or language facilitation to achieve. This in turn is linked to expected prices and perhaps delivery time. Some clients accept poor translations, which are matched with a reduced price and an increased speed as typically demonstrated by MT-based outputs, which are fast, often free and suffer from inconsistent quality. As we observed, this tends to occur with Receiver-commissioned translation work. This is the market that accepts less-than-perfect translations at a low cost.

The quality issues also relate to a multi-level language facilitation, as one example of language management discussed in Chapter 5. In conventional translation, unedited translations, perhaps required urgently, are marked as draft translations. In a similar way, translations produced by MT are sometimes labeled as such. Automated subtitles used by NHK (Nihon Hoso Kyokai – Japan Broadcast Corporation) for certain news items are accompanied by a disclaimer stating that the subtitles were computer generated. The definition of 'quality' is increasingly influenced by the end use of the given translation, as specified by the client. In particular, new types of Message such as Web sites or CD multimedia products now demand quality judged not only in terms of Content but also Package. In the case of extensive adaptation, quality judged against fidelity to the source text will be out of context and irrelevant. In such instances, quality is something to be judged by user specifications, and yet such specifications have been lacking in conventional translation. Melby (1995) discusses such concepts and suggests that user specifications may include such details as user terminology and how to handle the case of exceptions. With increasing sophistication at the user end, solutions such as language management and globalization strategies, and with such tools as Translation Memory, Translation quality may become precisely specifiable by the user.

Issue of machine-assisted production

Conventional language facilitation was entirely dependent on human efforts. This has changed drastically owing to the development of technology, which has significantly influenced the production of translation although it has not yet had the same impact on interpretation. Today's translation competence includes the proficient use of technology. For example, certain Messages created in digital environments are impossible to process without the use of technology at some point in the translation. Also, some clients are rightly or wrongly making the use of technology such as TM by the translation provider compulsory, and look on the lack of technology in the production process as lack of translation competence. Although full automation is not achieved in most translation production, machine-assisted translation is now a norm in the sense that technology facilitates most aspects of the translation process.

The question of how much more the computer will encroach into the translation and interpretation processes often causes heated arguments, particularly among human translators and interpreters. This is the debate regarding whether or not computers can ever replace human language facilitators. Philosophically, the most difficult factor involved in Translation using a computer system is quantifying the nature of human-to-human communication, the human ability to express motivations by using language in many creative ways, albeit within the confines of the language system. Unless the computer can identify the human agent's motivation behind the text, such a program is likely to run into the walls of separate language systems. The process of translation and interpretation can be regarded as seeing through the common human intention embedded in a different language system in its activation. But does it take a human to pick up this often-elusive human motivation embedded in text and speech?

One clear future for human translators and interpreters is that they will need to accept the likelihood of increasing IT application to their work and that this continuum will advance in the direction of machines that are able to detect the human agent's motivation behind the text and speech. However, the way the machine processes such information will probably be different from the way that humans do. In the meantime, human agents are more likely to adapt their inputs to suit the computer system, and this process may gradually be automated.

One should be able to see from our discussion that, in order to go global and operate in a global information society, the importance of languages in communications of every variety looms large. To function as a global citizen implies acquiring new knowledge about language, culture and multilingual communication, and the tools and technologies required to support them. This is true of businessmen and all other players on the global scene, not only the teletranslator and the teleinterpreter. Of course, the latter are the experts in providing Translation services, but the former need to know 'what they are getting into,' if they are to become as aware as possible of the nature of multilingual communication.

Conclusions

We have explored the implication for Translation of the fundamental change in the communications infrastructure as provided by global communications networks. We have presented our subjective perspective of emerging patterns in the area of translation and interpretation with a vision of the new paradigm as teletranslation and teleinterpretation. As we have admitted at the beginning, we do not have a crystal ball and this is only our interpretation supported to a degree by some experts' views of the direction of technological developments. One of the fascinating abilities that human beings have is creativity, which often appears in unpredictable ways. This same creativity is also what makes our language difficult to process by means of a computer. It is quite possible that new innovations might come from something we have never imagined or are simply unimaginable from the current vantage point. However, we hope that the concept of teletranslation and teleinterpretation has given readers food for thought and will create useful debate to further crystallize the future of these important professions. These actions themselves affect the way the future turns out.

Topics for Further Research or Discussion

(1) Try to think of examples of language mediation such as subtitling that went terribly wrong with mismatched 'frame' and 'scenes'?

(2) If it is possible to provide nonverbal communication mediation/ translation, when is it desirable and when not? If it is done, how could it be managed?

Notes

1. This part draws heavily on an unpublished doctoral thesis (O'Hagan, 2000b).

Postscript

Globalization is now a fact of life for many societies and organizations, regardless of the moral questions it sometimes seems to raise. Of course translators and interpreters have always facilitated globalization (without it being regarded as such) by localizing all kinds of communications between the Sender and the Receiver of the Message whenever a direct communication is not possible between them. Without input from screen translators, Hollywood films will not sell outside of English-speaking countries. Without interpreters, certain international exchanges and negotiations cannot take place either face to face or via other communications media. Similarly, computer software companies have come to rely on localizers to create a given user environment specified by the language and associated cultural conventions of the market. Seen in this way, translators and interpreters are an essential cog in the globalization process.

The 'meme'[1] of internationalization is beginning to spread beyond the working environment of the language worker. It reflects the awareness that a readership extends beyond the initial language of the sender/writer.

The Booker Prize author Kazuo Ishiguro suggests that he belongs to a new generation of writers of English who take translation difficulties into consideration when they write, knowing their books will be published in different languages (Asahi, 2001). This is an internationalization process undertaken at source during the creation of the message. While it cannot overcome all language problems, internationalization certainly facilitates subsequent translation and localization. Translators and interpreters can also contribute to this pre-translation process by applying their cross-cultural and cross-lingual knowledge and expertise.

Culture always matters for translation and interpretation, as it does with globalization. Take as an example a recent move to locate in India, where there is a large population of English speakers, call centers serving American markets. But speaking English is not itself considered sufficient and so the Indian operators are assigned American-sounding names to introduce themselves to customers, and furthermore are required to familiarize themselves with popular American soap operas such as *Friends* and *Ally McBeal* so that they can participate in small talk with American callers. This is part of culturalization. When the 'location' loses significance, not only language but also cultural knowledge is highlighted as a communication tool.

A few decades from now, language engineering will bear some fruit in producing efficient production tools such as super translation memory for language professionals, while at the same time providing an increased level of automation of language support for users of various communications devices. Such engineering solutions will no doubt be further augmented by the human effort of making the communication amenable to translation and localization. Indeed, the future of multilingual language support may lie in an approach based on IA (Intelligence Augmentation)[2] rather than in the direction sought by hardcore AI (Artificial Intelligence).

With the constantly changing communications landscape, the language industry now more than at any other time needs to invest in the education of language professionals who can serve the future needs that will arise from further globalization and the advancement of communications technologies. It is our hope that this book has in some way facilitated readers to rethink translation and interpretation and how we communicate globally.

September 11, 2001

The catastrophic events of this day bring home the desperate need for better communication among all peoples. As stated by Hanan Ashrawi[3], a popular leader in Palestine and a chief participant in negotiations with Israel, it is essential to be able to reach the source of discontent among peoples and understand it in order to begin a dialogue that may placate the hostility. To be successful, this will obviously entail the facilitation of multilingual communication and, above all, understanding across cultures. At the same time, these events have triggered an increased interest in communication in cyberspace, and a reluctance to rely on conventional means of transportation to bring people together. This could imply greater reliance on the use of teletranslation, teleinterpretation and Translation-mediated Communication in the coming years.

Notes

1. A meme is a unit of imitation. Richard Dawkins (1976: 192) introduced the term and the concepts of memes, which are like genes and 'propagate themselves in the meme pool by leaping from brain to brain.' Chesterman (2000) in his *Memes of Translation* discusses how memes of translation theory have spread historically.
2. This is an approach conceptualized by Pattie Maes of MIT Media Lab.
3. A television interview with Peter Jennings of ABC News, September 15, 2001.

References

Abaitua, J. (1999) Is it worth learning translation technology? *Training Translators and Interpreters: New Directions for the Millenium*. Third Forum on Translation in Vic, May 12–15. Universitat de Vic, Spain (http://www.serv-inf.deusto.es/abaitua/konzeptu/ta/vic.htm).

Ananthaswamy, A. (2000) Being there. *New Scientist* 2261, 52–55.

Argyle, M. (1988) *Bodily Communication* (2nd edn). London: Methuen & Co Ltd.

Asahi (2001). Kazuo Ishiguro talks about his new masterpiece. 2 May, 20.

Ashworth, D. (1997) Transterpreting: A new modality for interpreting on the Internet. Paper presented at the PPDLA (Pan-Pacific Distance Learning Association) Conference, Honolulu, Hawaii.

Bell, R.T. (1991) *Translation and Translating: Theory and Practice*. London: Longman.

Berners-Lee, T., Hendler, J. and Lassila, O. (2001) The semantic web. *Scientific American* May, 29–37 (also at http://www.scientificamerican.com/2001/0501issue/0501berners-lee.html).

Bowers, J., Pycock, J. and O'Brien, J. (1996) Talk and embodiment in collaborative virtual environments. *Computer Human Interface 96 Electronic Proceedings* (http://www.acm.org/sigchi/chi96/proceedings/papers/Bowers/jb_txt.htm).

Brooks, D. (2000) What price globalization? Managing costs at Microsoft. In R.C. Sprung (ed.) *Translating into Success* (pp. 43–58). Amsterdam, Philadelphia: John Benjamins Publishing.

Brown, P. and Levinson, S.C. (1987) *Politeness: Some Universals in Language Usage*. Cambridge: Cambridge University Press.

Brutzman, D. (1997) Graphics internetworking: Bottlenecks and breakthroughs. In C. Dodsworth (ed.) *Digital Illusion* (pp. 61–96). Reading, MA: Addison-Wesley.

Cheng, S. (2000) Globalizing an e-commerce web site. In R.C. Sprung (ed.) *Translating into Success* (pp. 29–42). Amsterdam, Philadelphia: John Benjamins Publishing.

Chesterman, A. (2000) *Memes of Translation*. Amsterdam, Philadelphia: John Benjamins Publishing.

Collot, M. and Bellmore, N. (1996) Electronic language: A new variety of English. In S.C. Herring (ed.) *Computer-Mediated Communication: Linguistics, Social and Cross-cultural Perspectives*. Amsterdam, Philadelphia: John Benjamins Publishing.

Connell, T. (1999) Web support for distance learning in the field of translation. *ReCALL* 11(2), 31–7 (also at http://www.hull.ac.uk/cti/eurocall/recall/rvol11no2.pdf).

Corn, D. (2000) Filegate.gov. *Wired* November (online archive at http://www.wired.com/wired/archive/8.11/govdocs.html).

Crystal, D. (1997) *English as a Global Language*. Cambridge: Cambridge University Press.

Database (1998). *Time Digital* 4, 18 May.

Dawkins, R. (1976) *The Selfish Gene.* Oxford: Oxford University Press.

Day, R. (1996) Are translating and interpreting drawing together? *Proceedings of the XIV World Congress of the Federation Internationale des Traducteurs (FIT)* Vol.2 (pp. 940–45). Melbourne: AUSIT (The Australian Institute of Interpreters and Translators).

De Groot, A.M.B. (1997) The cognitive study of translation and interpretation. In J.H. Danks, G.M. Shreve, S.B. Fountain and M.K. McBeath (eds) *Cognitive Processes in Translation and Interpreting* (pp. 25–56). Thousand Oaks: Sage Publications.

Dertouzos, M. (1997) *What Will Be: How the New World of Information Will Change Our Lives.* New York: HarperEdge.

Donath, J.S. (1997) Inhabiting the virtual city: The design of social environment for electronic communities. PhD thesis, MIT Media Lab (http://judith.www. media.mit.edu/Thesis).

Ekman, P. and Friesen, W. (1972) *Emotion in the Human Face: Guidelines for Research and an Integration of Findings.* New York: Pergamon Press.

Esselink, B (2000a) *A Practical Guide to Software Localization.* Amsterdam, Philadelphia: John Benjamins Publishing.

Esselink, B. (2000b) The technology game. *Language International* 12 (6), 20–22.

Fillmore, C.J. (1977) Scenes-and-frames semantics. In A. Zampolli (ed.) *Linguistic Structures Processing* (pp. 55–82). Amsterdam: North-Holland Publishing.

Flanagan, M. (1997) Machine translation of interactive texts. *Machine Translation Summit VI Proceedings* (p. 50). Washington, DC: AMTA.

Fry, D. (1998) Refreshing the parts translation can't reach: The rise of localization. *Proceedings of the Third Equivalences Conference Equivalences 97* (pp. 147–56). Bern: Association Suisse des Traducteurs, Terminologues et Interpreters (ASTTI).

Fry, D. (1999) Mission critical. *Language International* 11 (2), pp. 24 ff.

Fry, D. (2000) Upping the ante. *Language International* 12 (4), pp. 12 ff.

Gile, D. (1995) *Basic Concepts and Models for Interpreter and Translator Training.* Amsterdam, Philadelphia: John Benjamins Publishing.

Hadfield, P. (2000) Sayonara WAP. *New Scientist* 2261, 39–41.

Hall, E.T. (1976) *Beyond Culture.* New York: Doubleday.

Halliday, M.A.K. (1989) *Spoken and Written Language* (2nd edn). Oxford: Oxford University Press.

Hatim, B. and Mason, I. (1997) *The Translator as Communicator.* London: Routledge.

Heim, M. (1987) *Electric Language: A Philosophical Study of Word Processing.* New Haven: Yale University Press.

Herring, S. (1996) Introduction. In S. Herring (ed.) *Computer-mediated Communication: Linguistics, Social and Cross-cultural Perspectives.* Amsterdam, Philadelphia: John Benjamins Publishing.

Hiltz, S.R. and Turoff, M. (1993) *The Network Nation* (rev. edn). Cambridge, MA: MIT Press.

Homnack, M. (2000) The future of globalization technology: Is it the graveyard? *Localization Industry Standards Association (LISA) Newsletter* 9 (4).

Hopkins, J.D. (2001) Unto every nation, kindred, tongue and people. *Localization Industry Standards Association (LISA) Newsletter* X 2, 14–17.

Hornberger, J.C., Gibson, C.D., Jr, Wood, W., Dequeldre, C., Corso, I., Palla, B. and Bloch, D.A. (1996) Eliminating language barriers for non-English-speaking patients. *Medical Care* 34 (8), 845–56.

Hutchins, J. (1999) Retrospect and prospect in computer-based translation. *Proceedings of Machine Translation Summit VII 99* (pp. 30–36). Asia-Pacific Association for Machine Translation (AAMT).

Inggs, J. (2000) Comment on 'Translation technology' in *Translate2000* February 29 (http://www.translat2000.com/discussion/Judith-technology.htm).

Irmler, U. (2001) The University of Washington presents a new certificate program in localization. *Language International* 13 (2), 20–22.

JCTV implementing translation (1997) *Nihon Kogyo Shinbun* (Japan Industries paper), January 30, section 7.

Jeanty, R. (1997) The future of the localization industry. *Localization Industry Standards Association (LISA) Newsletter* 6 (2), 7–11.

Joscelyne, A. (1999) Millennium-ready? *Language International* 11 (6), 31–33.

Joscelyne, A. (2000) The role of translation in an international organization. In R.C. Sprung (ed.) *Translating into Success* (pp. 81–95). Amsterdam, Philadelphia: John Benjamins Publishing.

Kahney, L. (2000) The third-generation gap. *Scientific American* October, 42–45.

Kalawsky, R.S. (1993) *The Science of Virtual Reality and Virtual Environments*. Wokingham: Addison-Wesley Publishing Company.

Kay, M., Gawron, J.M. and Norvig, P. (1994) *Verbmobil*. CA: CSLI (Center for the Study of Language and Information).

Keynote (2001) With a little help from Hollywood Jeeves the Butler caters to Japanese needs. *Localization Industry Standards Association (LISA) Newsletter* X 2, 8–13.

Kingscott, A.G. (1996) Translation, the 21st century horizon. *The Proceedings of the XIV World Congress of the Federation Internationale des Traducteurs (FIT)* Vol.2 (pp. 816–26). Melbourne: AUSIT (The Australian Institute of Interpreters and Translators).

Kiraly, D. (2000a) *A Social Constructivist Approach to Translator Education*. Manchester, UK: St Jerome Publishing.

Kiraly, D. (2000b) From teacher-oriented to learning-centered classrooms in translator education: Control, chaos or collaboration? Innovation in translator and interpreter training position paper (http://www.fut.es/~apym/symp/kiraly.html).

Kremer, B. (1997) Interpreting: Quantifying quality. *Language International* 9.1, pp. 33 ff.

Kuhn, T.S. (1962) *The Structure of Scientific Revolutions*. Chicago: University of Chicago Press.

Kurz, I. (1996) Special features of media interpreting as seen by interpreters and users. *The Proceedings of the XIV World Congress of the Federation Internationale des Traducteurs (FIT)* Vol.2 (pp. 957–65). Melbourne: AUSIT (The Australian Institute of Interpreters and Translators).

LETRAC (1998) Background and Market Situation (http://www.iai.uni-sb.de/LETRAC/letrac-data.html#GR).

LISA (2000) *The Localization Industry Primer*. Fechy: Localization Industry Standards Association (LISA).

Lockwood, R. (1998) Language technologies and technical communication opportunities in FP5. *Computing & Control Engineering Journal* 9 (6), 253–56.

Lockwood, R. (1999) You snooze, you lose. *Language International* 11 (4), 12–14.

Lommel, A. (2001) Unicode and OpenType. *Localization Industry Standards Association (LISA) Newsletter* X 2.

Lunde, K. (1993) *Understanding Japanese Information Processing*. CA: O'Reilly & Associates, Inc.

Maia, B. (2000) Translation technology. *Translate2000* January 19 (http://www.translat2000.com/discussion/TransTechnology.htm).

Malinowski, B. (1967) *The Language of Magic and Gardening*. Indiana: Indiana University Press.

Marvin, L.E. (1995) Spoof, spam, lurk and lag: The aesthetics of text-based virtual realities. *Journal of Computer-Mediated Communication* 1, 2.

Massaro, D.W. and Moser-Mercer, B. (1996) Editorial. *Interpreting* 1 (1), 1–6.

Matsunaga, M. (2000) *i-mode Jiken* [The i-mode Affair]. Tokyo: Kadokawa.

McLuhan, M. (1994) *Understanding Media: The Extensions of Man*. Cambridge, MA: MIT Press.

Melby, A. (1995) *The Possibility of Language*. Amsterdam, Philadelphia: John Benjamins Publishing.

Mintz, D. (1998) Hold the phone: Telephone interpreting scrutinized. *PROTEUS* (the Digital Edition of the quarterly Newsletter of the National Association of Judiciary Interpreters and Translators) Winter, 7 (1).

Moser-Mercer, B. (1997) Beyond curiosity: Can interpreting research meet the challenge? In J.H. Danks, G.M. Shreve, S.B. Fountain and M.K. McBeath (eds) *Cognitive Processes in Translation and Interpreting* (pp. 176–195). Thousand Oaks: Sage Publications.

Mouzourakis, P. (1996) Videoconferencing: Techniques and challenges. *Interpreting* 1 (1), 21–38.

Negroponte, N. (1995) *Being Digital*. Cambridge, MA: MIT Press.

Nida, E.A. and Taber, C. (1969) *The Theory and Practice of Translation*. Leiden: E.J. Brill.

Nielsen, J. (1999) *Designing Web Usability*. Indiana: New Riders.

Nishigaki, T. (1999) What can MT do for multilingualism on the Net? *Proceedings of Machine Translation Summit VII 99* (pp. 15–20). Asia-Pacific Association for Machine Translation (AAMT).

O'Hagan, M. (1996) *The Coming Industry of Teletranslation*. Clevedon: Multilingual Matters.

O'Hagan, M. (1997) Prelude to a new QA era for the translation industry. *Localization Industry Standards Association (LISA) Newsletter* 5 (4), 15–19.

O'Hagan, M. (1999) The making of translators on the Web. *Localization Industry Standards Association (LISA) Newsletter* 8 (4), 23–26.

O'Hagan, M. (2000a) E-commerce Japanese style and the implication for localization. *Localization Industry Standards Association (LISA) Newsletter* 9 (2).

O'Hagan, M. (2000b) Hypertransterpretation in HyperReality. Unpublished PhD thesis, Victoria University of Wellington, New Zealand.

Ong, W.J. (1982) *Orality and Literacy: The Technologizing of the Word*. London: Methuen.

Oviatt, S.L. and Cohen, P.R. (1992). Spoken language in interpreted telephone dialogues. *Computer Speech and Language* 6 (3), 277–302.

Ozolins, U. (1991) Interpreting, translating and language policy. Report to the Language and Society Centre National Languages Institute of Australia.

Palloff, R.M. and Pratt, K. (1999) *Building Learning Communities in Cyberspace*. San Francisco: Jossey-Bass Publishers.

'Products and systems' (1997) in *MT News International* 17, 4.

Rheingold, H. (1995) *The Virtual Community*. London: Minerva.

Rice, A. (n.d.) An essay on the Web and translation (http://www.crossroads.net/a/writing/webtrans.html).

Sachs, A. (2000) Boo! How he startled the book world. *Time* March 27, 42.

Sager, J. (1993) *Language Engineering and Translation: Consequences of Automation*. Amsterdam, Philadelphia: John Benjamins Publishing.

Sakamura, K. (1995) Multilingual computing as a global communications infrastructure. *Proceedings of 12th TRON Project International Symposium* (pp. 2–14).

Schäffner, C. (ed.) (2000) *Translation in the Global Village*. Clevedon: Multilingual Matters.

Schmitt, E. (2000) *The Multilingual Site Blueprint*. Cambridge, MA: Forrester Research.

Schrage, M. (1990) *Shared Minds: The New Technology of Collaboration*. New York: Random House.

Schrage, M. (1995*) No More Teams! Mastering the Dynamics of Creative Collaboration*. New York: Doubleday-Dell Publishing Company.

Schwartz, P. (1996) *The Art of the Long View: Path to Strategic Insight for Yourself and Your Company*. Sydney: Prospect Publishing.

Seleskovitch, D. (1994) *Interpreting for International Conferences* (2nd rev. edn). Washington, DC: Pen and Booth.

Shannon, C.E. and Weaver, W. (1949) *The Mathematical Theory of Communication*. Urbana: University of Illinois Press.

Snell-Hornby, M. (2000) Communicating in the global village: On language, translation and cultural identity. In C. Schäffner (ed.) *Translation in the Global Village* (pp. 11–28). Clevedon: Multilingual Matters.

Sugimoto, T. and Levin, J.A. (2000) Multiple literacies and multimedia: A comparison of Japanese and American uses of the Internet. In G.E. Hawisher and C.L. Selfe (eds) *Global Literacies and the World-Wide Web* (pp. 133–53). London, New York: Routledge.

Susskind, R. (1996) *The Future of Law: Facing the Challenges of Information Technology*. New York: Oxford University Press.

Tanaka, H. (1999) What should we do next for MT system development? *Proceedings of Machine Translation Summit VII 99* (pp. 3–8). Asia-Pacific Association for Machine Translation (AAMT).

Terashima, N. (1995a) *Multimedia to Joho Superhighway: Multimedia and Information Superhighway*. Tokyo: HBJ Publishing.

Terashima, N. (1995b) HyperReality. *Proceedings of the International Conference on Recent Advances in Mechatronics (ICRAM)* (pp. 621–26). Istanbul, Turkey: ICRAM.

'The Doctor is in' (1998) Language Engineering gets a powerful new advocate. *Language International* 10.2, 40–41.

The Economist (2001a) The shape of phones to come. The technology quarterly, 24 March, p. 20.

The Economist (2001b) The cutting edge of virtual reality. The technology quarterly, 24 March, pp. 30–32.

The Futures Group (1994) *Scenarios*. A publication of the United Nations Development Program's African Futures Project in collaboration with the United Nations University's Millennium Project Feasibility Study: Phase II.

Tiffin, J. and Rajasingham, L. (1995) *In Search of the Virtual Class*. London: Routledge.

Tiffin, J. and Rajasingham, L. (2001) The hyperclass. In J. Tiffin and N. Terashima (eds) *HyperReality: Paradigm for the Third Millennium*. New York and London: Routledge.

Torres del Rey, J. (2000) On translation technology: Comments on Belinda Maia's paper. In *Translate2000* February 29 (http://www.translat2000.com/discussion/Jesus-technology.htm).

Van der Heijden, K. (1996) *Scenarios: The Art of Strategic Conversation*. Chester: John Wiley & Sons.

Venuti, L. (1995) *The Translator's Invisibility: A History of Translation*. London: Routledge.

Vermeer, H. (1992) Describing nonverbal behavior in the Odyssey: Scenes and verbal frames as translation problems. In F. Poyatos (ed.) *Advances in Nonverbal Communication* (pp. 285–300). Amsterdam, Philadelphia: John Benjamins Publishing.

Viaggio, S. (1997a) Kinesics and the simultaneous interpreter: The advantages of listening with one's eyes and speaking with one's body. In F. Poyatos (ed.) *Nonverbal Communication and Translation* (pp. 283–94). Amsterdam, Philadelphia: John Benjamins Publishing.

Viaggio, S. (1997b) Translation and interpretation: Essence and training basics. Fourth seminar organized by Translation and Editorial Service, United Nations office, Vienna International Centre.

Vidal, M. (1998) Telephone interpreting: Technological advances or due process impediment? In *PROTEUS* (the Digital Edition of the quarterly Newsletter of the National Association of Judiciary Interpreters and Translators) Summer 7 (3).

Waldrop, M.M. and Jensen, K. (2001) Emerging technologies that will change the world (http://www.technologyreview.com/magazine/jan01/tr10_jensen.asp).

Wang, G. and Dordick, H.S. (1993) *The Information Society: A Retrospective View*. Thousand Oaks: Sage Publications.

Warschauer, M. (1999) *Electronic Literacies*. Mahwah, NJ: Erlbaum.

Webb, J. and Graham-Rowe, D. (2000) Everything, anywhere. *New Scientist* 2261, 33–35.

Werry, C.C. (1996) Linguistic and interactional features of internet relay chat. In S. Herring (ed.) *Computer-Mediated Communication: Linguistic, Social and Cross-Cultural Perspectives* (pp. 47–63). Amsterdam, Philadelphia: John Benjamins Publishing.

Wilss, W. (1996) *Knowledge and Skills in Translator Behaviour*. Amsterdam, Philadelphia: John Benjamins Publishing.

Index